CHAMPIONS AGAIN!

CHAMPIONS AGAIN!

KEITH ERICKSON

THOMAS NELSON PUBLISHERS
Nashville • Atlanta • London • Vancouver

Published in Nashville, Tennessee, by Thomas Nelson, Inc., and distributed in Canada by Word Communications, Ltd., Richmond, British Columbia, and in the United Kingdom by Word (UK), Ltd., Milton Keynes, England.

Scripture quotations are from the NEW KING JAMES VERSION of the Bible. Copyright © 1979, 1980, 1982, 1990, 1994, Thomas Nelson, Inc., Publishers.

Library of Congress Cataloging-in-Publication Data

Erickson, Keith, 1944-
    Champions again! / Keith Erickson.
      p. cm.
    ISBN 0-7852-7519-3 (pbk.)
    1. UCLA Bruins (Basketball team) 2. University of California, Los Angeles—basketball. I. Title.
GV885.43.C34E75   1996
796.323'63'0979494—dc20   95-47682
                                                       CIP

Printed in the United States of America

1 2 3 4 5 6 7 - 02 01 00 99 98 97 96

This book is dedicated to my whole family, from Ruthie and Ray on down, but especially to my son, Sean, who nearly didn't make it after three surgeries while this book was being done.

Don't ever forget the Lord who brought you through it!

Contents

Foreword

Because Keith Erickson was such a vital force in the first two of UCLA's NCAA championship basketball teams of 1963-64 and 1964-65, it is quite logical that he be involved in the writing of *Champions Again!*

Keith finished UCLA in 1965 but has maintained a close relationship with the university and with basketball in all the ensuing years. He had a fine pro career with the Phoenix Suns and the Los Angeles Lakers, served as commentator for both the Lakers and the Suns, has produced a number of motivational tapes, and has been a model of Christian leadership to our youth for many years.

The title *Champions Again!* aptly describes the 1994-95 UCLA Bruins (although they have had a number of outstanding teams in the last twenty years), as this was the first time they attained true championship stature since the 1974-75 season.

UCLA sports fans, as well as others who enjoy and follow intercollegiate basketball, will thoroughly enjoy this reminiscent treatise on UCLA basketball over the last three decades.

John Wooden
UCLA (Retired)

Acknowledgments

What a joy it was to spend time remembering the good old days with good friends with better memories than mine.

Thank you, Coach Wooden and Coach Norman, Walt Hazzard, and Bill Walton.

And thanks to all of the people who helped in the UCLA athletic department, especially Bill Bennett.

And special thanks to the relief pitcher, Thomas Bonk, who came in from the bullpen to clean things up.

—K.E.

Destined to Be Champions

1

Inspiration is where you find it, which may be an odd way of saying that some of the greatest lessons in life are learned in places you might not expect. Your mom told you not to touch the stove, but if you did anyway, you probably never touched it again. It's the same in sports. Sometimes you learn a lot more about yourself when you get burned.

And sometimes you learn how to win because you lost. It's not as strange as it sounds. As a matter of fact, there are at least two NCAA basketball championship banners hanging as evidence in Pauley Pavilion at UCLA. Since losing is about as satisfying as dribbling a basketball off your foot, the 1995 UCLA Bruins men's team had learned something from the year before, just as the 1964 team had learned the same thing years earlier.

Make no mistake about it, the 1995 Bruins knew all about their history lesson.

In the 1994 NCAA tournament, the Bruins embarrassed themselves by losing to the University of Tulsa 112-102 in the first round. After this painful loss, UCLA star forward Ed O'Bannon was determined that in his senior year things would not end so poorly. O'Bannon called a meeting of his teammates and told them how strongly he felt. He challenged everyone to concentrate on playing together as a team in 1995.

More than thirty years earlier in 1963, I experienced the same feelings after being similarly humiliated by Arizona State in the NCAA Regionals. Our coach, John Wooden, was encouraged, though, because we had gained invaluable experience playing together, and all five starters would be back the next year.

He was right to have been encouraged. We won it all in 1964—the first of ten national championships UCLA would win under Coach Wooden.

But what was to happen as these latter-day Bruins were to begin their season in the fall of 1994? Here's a brief look at the 1995 UCLA Bruins.

ED O'BANNON

(SENIOR FORWARD, 6'8"/217 POUNDS)

Ed became a Bruin in 1990, when the team with which he originally signed a letter of intent, the University of Nevada at Las Vegas (UNLV), was punished by the

NCAA for recruiting violations. Ed then chose UCLA because of its basketball tradition and because it was close to home in Lakewood, California, where he and his brother, Charles, had starred at Artesia High School.

In his freshman year at UCLA, Ed tore the anterior cruciate ligament (ACL) in his left knee. It is a potentially career-ending injury. During the five-hour surgery his ACL was replaced by an Achilles tendon from a cadaver. Through conditioning and weight training, he eventually recovered from the injury and pushed himself relentlessly to come back as strong as before.

Ed received the Coach John Wooden Award as the team's most valuable player after the 1994 season. He had scored 30 points in thirty-seven minutes against Tulsa in the 112-102 season-ending loss. It was from that humiliating loss that Ed challenged his teammates to play with pride the following season. Ed O'Bannon is the leader of the team!

CHARLES O'BANNON

(SOPHOMORE FORWARD, 6'6½"/205 POUNDS)

The younger and more outgoing of the high-flying O'Bannon brothers, Charles was one of the nation's most highly recruited high school players in 1993. Charles was considering Kentucky, Michigan, UCLA, and arch rival USC before deciding to join Ed with the Bruins. After he signed his letter of intent, Ed reportedly said to Charles, "Let's go win a national championship."

Charles is a coach's dream, loaded with talent, beloved by his teammates, a never-say-die competitor, and totally unselfish.

Charles and Ed's father, Ed Sr., had attended UCLA and was a wide receiver on the football team back in 1971.

TYUS EDNEY

(SENIOR POINT GUARD, 5'10"/152 POUNDS)

Tyus grew up with the O'Bannons in the Long Beach, California, area. He was leading playground teams with the O'Bannons when he and Ed were nine and Charles was seven.

Tyus was named the team's Most Valuable Player in 1993. He was a point guard on the bronze-medal winning team at the Goodwill Games in 1994, when he was also a *Basketball Times* Second-Team All-American.

Tyus, like Ed O'Bannon, is quiet and even-tempered. Despite all of his success, he is humble and coachable. He might be the quickest and fastest player in the country.

GEORGE ZIDEK

(SENIOR CENTER, 7'0"/250 POUNDS)

When the Bruin coaches were unable to recruit local high school star Cherokee Parks, they went after George Zidek, who had played extensively for the Czech Republic national team. George made quantum leaps in his four

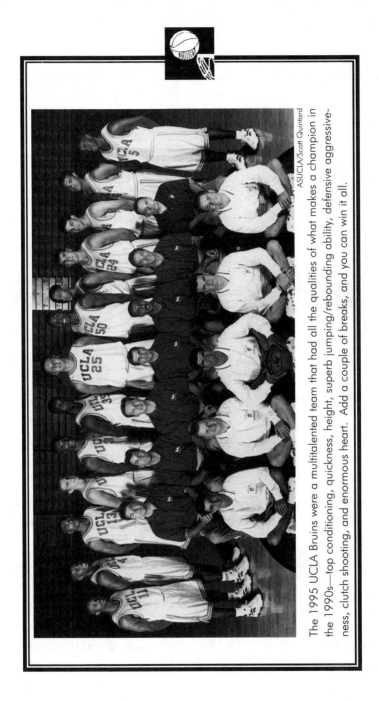

ASUCLA/Scott Quintard

The 1995 UCLA Bruins were a multitalented team that had all the qualities of what makes a champion in the 1990s—top conditioning, quickness, height, superb jumping/rebounding ability, defensive aggressiveness, clutch shooting, and enormous heart. Add a couple of breaks, and you can win it all.

years at UCLA as his desire grew and his tremendous work ethic began to pay off.

The 7'0" George and the 5'10" Tyus Edney formed a true "odd couple" when they roomed together their first two years as Bruins. George is an outstanding student and was a 1994 GTE Second-Team Academic All-American. He is considered a classic traditional center with the best hook shot at UCLA since Kareem Abdul-Jabbar.

"TOBY" (JOHN GARFIELD) BAILEY
(FRESHMAN GUARD, 6'5"/185 POUNDS)

Recruited to replace Shon Tarver, the shooting guard who switched to UCLA from UNLV with Ed O'Bannon, Toby played ball at Loyola High in Los Angeles. Toby has high energy, plays with passion, is a spectacular leaper, and is seemingly oblivious to pressure. He was a *USA Today* Honorable Mention Prep All-American Player. His teammates love his personality and his hilarious impressions of them.

CAMERON DOLLAR
(SOPHOMORE POINT GUARD, 6'1"/173 POUNDS)

This Atlanta native played ball at St. John's Prospect High School in Frederick, Maryland. Cameron doesn't have the physical abilities of a Michael Jordan, but he does what they call "intangibles" on the court. He is a tenacious defender, an emotional spark plug, and an intense leader out on the floor. Of all his teammates, he has the utmost level of confidence. In high school, he was voted *Sporting News* Prep Player of the Year in 1993.

"J. R." (MILTON JR.) HENDERSON

(FRESHMAN FORWARD, 6'9"/215 POUNDS)

J. R. was a *USA Today* Honorable Mention All-American at East Bakersfield High School, California, where he averaged more than 27 points per game. Stoic in demeanor on the court, J. R. leads by example, not by emotion. He can play all five positions. Multitalented!

KRIS JOHNSON

(FRESHMAN FORWARD, 6'4"/220 POUNDS)

Kris was L.A. City High School Player of the Year as a junior at Crenshaw High School in Los Angeles. His father, Marques, who played for UCLA in the mid-seventies, was one of the best Bruins of them all. Kris has enormous ability and potential and should bloom just the way his father did.

OMM'A GIVENS

(FRESHMAN CENTER, 6'10"/235 POUNDS)

After playing for Aberdeen High School in Aberdeen, Washington, omm'A was one of the most highly recruited players in America in 1994. omm'A is upbeat, has great potential, practices hard every day, and could be a real player. He was a McDonald's High School All-American.

IKE NWANKWO

(SOPHOMORE CENTER, 6'11"/234 POUNDS)

Ike was nominated to the McDonald's High School All-American Team when he played at Cypress Creek in Houston. Born in Lansing, Michigan, his parents are both from Nigeria. He would like to be a lawyer one day and is therefore affectionately known to his teammates as "Johnnie Cochran."

KEVIN DEMPSEY

(JUNIOR FORWARD, 6'6"/210 POUNDS)

Kevin averaged 26 points per game in high school in San Jose, California. A fine shooter who has been plagued by injuries, Kevin's tongue-in-cheek goals are to shoot like Larry Bird, pass like Magic Johnson, and jump like Michael Jordan.

BOB MYERS

(SOPHOMORE FORWARD, 6'6"/210 POUNDS)

Bob played his high school ball at Monte Vista High School in Danville, California. Teammates call him Forrest Gump because as a walk-on (which means he was not recruited and had no scholarship), he has played on an NCAA championship team, been to the White House, met the president, been a part of one of the most watched events of the year, and received a full scholarship for his dedication, attitude, and work ethic.

Coached by Jim Harrick, who was assisted by Mark Gottfried, Lorenzo Romar, and Steve Lavin, the 1995 Bruins appeared to have all the talent necessary to make a run at the national championship. With a competitive fire burning brightly in the gut of team leaders Ed O'Bannon and Tyus Edney, might this be the year that brings basketball glory back to the place where an incredible dynasty began in 1964, with a bunch of guys who were "too small" to win the NCAA title?

How to Build a Championship Team

2

The 1963-64 UCLA basketball team had a brilliant, undefeated season, going 30-0. You'll be surprised to hear how this team was assembled. It was a puzzle of rather unlikely pieces.

FRED SLAUGHTER

Fred was a muscular 6'5", 230-pound track star from Kansas. He ran the 100 in ten seconds flat and won the state discus title as a senior at Topeka High School. He played only six games of the basketball season his senior year because of a broken shoulder.

Fred was not recruited by either Kansas or Kansas State. After a divorce, his mother moved to Los Angeles. She worked for a UCLA fan who called Assistant Coach Jerry Norman to tell of a

youngster who was "big, strong, and fast." Neither Coach Wooden nor Norman had seen Fred play. So sight unseen, with no idea how good a basketball player he was, Fred was recruited to join the Bruins and piece number one was set in place.

JACK HIRSCH

Jack was a center in high school in the San Fernando Valley before going to junior college for two years. At 6'3", he didn't jump well, couldn't run very fast, and had a limited shooting range. But he was an outstanding defensive player with a nose for the ball. He was a solid, but not spectacular, player.

Jack's family was wealthy, so he could have attended any school he chose. But his father wanted him to go to UCLA to get a solid education. No one else was breaking down the Hirsch door to recruit Jack, and Coach Norman hadn't seen him play for two years, so to please his dad, Jack signed up at UCLA. Piece number two was in place.

WALT HAZZARD

Walt grew up on the East Coast, playing in gyms and playgrounds with older, more experienced collegiate and professional players in the area. He went to the same Philadelphia high school (Overbrook) as outstanding basketball players Wilt Chamberlain, Wayne Hightower, and Wally Jones.

ASCULA

John Wooden, one of the most successful coaches ever, with a remarkable lifetime winning percentage of .813, was more intense on the bench than many people realized. He always had that tightly rolled program in his hand.

Willie Nalls, a former Bruin who at the time was playing in the NBA with the Boston Celtics, saw the young Hazzard holding his own with the older guys and called Coach Norman to tell him he'd "found a player."

Walt went to a southern California junior college for a year and then entered UCLA. He was a wizard with the ball, a "Magic Johnson" before his time. He could pass and handle the ball like a pro, and he also had a confidence and intensity that was contagious. He was the self-appointed spokesman for the team. Although our coaches had never seen Walt play before they recruited him, piece number three was signed up on a tip from Nalls.

GAIL GOODRICH

Gail was next. His father had been the captain of the USC basketball team in 1939 and was disappointed that the Trojans were not interested in his son. Gail had a good senior year, but he was so small that his advancement to the next level was in doubt.

In the city tournament he was outstanding, and all of a sudden USC was interested. But Gail Sr. was furious and wouldn't let his son even consider them. Gail graduated in midyear, and before Gail or his father could change their minds, he was in class in Westwood. As a 5'7" and 135-pound junior, of course, no one could predict if Gail would grow and continue to improve.

KEITH ERICKSON

I had not been offered a scholarship to any four-year school after high school, so my option was El Camino junior college, where it was my great fortune to play for one of Coach Wooden's former players, George Stanich.

At the end of that season (1961-62), Stanich called Coach Norman at UCLA to tell him he had a player who could help the Bruins.

"Who?" asked Norman. George said, "Keith Erickson."

My junior college team had played the Bruin freshmen that year, but Norman couldn't remember me. After reviewing the scorer's book for that game, he was not impressed when he saw "4 points and 3 rebounds" by my name. After much insistence by Stanich, though, Coach Norman agreed with the baseball coach, Art Reichle, that they would both offer me a half scholarship. Whichever team I made—baseball or basketball—would take over the whole ride. And if I made neither team, the coaches would lose only a half scholarship each. (Lots of confidence, huh?) I made the basketball team and became piece number five in the puzzle.

DOUG MCINTOSH

Doug had grown up in Kentucky. His parents moved to Los Angeles just before his senior year in high school, and they left him in Kentucky to finish up the year. He was being recruited by the head coach at the University of Tennessee, but the coach was fired before the next season. So the coach told his friend, John Wooden, about Doug.

In the meantime, Doug had joined his parents in L.A. Though he had never seen Doug play, on the word of a friend, Wooden brought him aboard. At least he was 6'6"—the tallest of all of us. He was also piece number six.

KENNY WASHINGTON

After Walt Hazzard's sophomore year at UCLA, he returned to Philadelphia for the summer and was impressed with a youngster from South Carolina who was playing ball in Philly. Walt called Coach Norman and told him of this "6'5" or 6'6" kid" who could shoot like Gary Cunningham (a great shooter who had just graduated), rebound like Slaughter, and "handle the ball like me" (Hazzard).

Just before school started in 1962, Coach Norman went down to the L.A. bus terminal with great anticipation to meet this young man who had come all the way from South Carolina. Looking for a big "6'5" or 6'6" kid," Norman was puzzled when no one fitting that description got off the bus. After much inquiry, he was introduced to a 6'3", 160-pound, skinny and shy Kenny Washington. Piece number seven had arrived.

ASUCLA

The first championship team in 1964. This photograph reveals our lack of height. All of the "tall guys" are standing up in the back row. Our reserve center, the big guy in the middle (6'8"), is the only one over 6'6".

Heading into the 1963-64 season, the seven players Coach Wooden would depend upon most were quite a group: one from Philadelphia, one from Kansas, one from South Carolina, and one from Kentucky. One so small that nobody else wanted him, one the wrong size and whom the coach hadn't seen play in two years, and one the coach couldn't even remember after seeing him play that same year!

Did this ragtag group have the makings of a championship team? Not likely! Certainly there were no Alcindors or Waltons in this group. But we were a team, and the brilliance of John Wooden was taking individual pieces and assembling them together to form a functioning whole.

In the early '60s, the UCLA basketball program was totally different from what it was to become—after the beautiful on-campus Pauley Pavilion was built and Lew Alcindor (Kareem Abdul-Jabbar)* led the Bruins to three straight NCAA championships. The total recruiting budget for the basketball program was five hundred dollars. Things were a lot cheaper back then, but you still couldn't go very far on five hundred bucks.

We practiced in the old men's gym, and through the

---

*Lew Alcindor, after his years at UCLA, took the name Kareem Abdul-Jabbar. To avoid confusion—except in an occasional quotation—I will use the name Kareem Abdul-Jabbar.

1961-62 season we still played a couple of games there. The gym held two thousand people in cramped and steamy quarters. It definitely provided a home-court advantage for the games, but the practices were like guerrilla warfare.

The court was on the third floor, with no air-conditioning and poor ventilation. Just behind the east-end basket, a curtain was pulled to keep the balls from disturbing the wrestling and gymnastics teams that worked out the same time we did. Coaches Wooden and Norman mopped the floor before practice every day, as Coach Wooden had done for seventeen years.

The locker facilities were in the basement, four levels below, and they were shared with students from gym classes, other UCLA teams, and the ROTC. We had no private dressing or shower areas.

Coach Wooden was meticulous about details. (The first lecture we received was on how to put on our socks and shoes and then properly tie our shoes to prevent blisters and injuries.) He met in the mornings with the other coaches and went over every aspect of practice for that day. His three-by-five note cards broke each three-hour practice down to the minute.

On the first day of practice in the fall, we started on fundamental drills. We ran those same monotonous drills until the last day of the season, thirty games later. To say that we were fundamentally sound would be a great understatement!

And the conditioning! We ran a full-court press for the

entire game, so to be in shape to play such a demanding defense for forty minutes, we ran from one drill to the next—right up to the last drill of the day.

Though we may have lacked in size, there's no doubt we were fundamentally sound, we were in tip-top shape, and we were a team—in every sense of the word.

John Wooden tells a story about a basketball coach from Czechoslovakia who spent time with the Bruins during that first championship season. The Czech coach had watched us practice and play. He was sitting with a group of people who were speculating on "who would win and why" before the NCAA championship game between UCLA and Duke.

Most people were saying that Duke would win because they had great individual players in Jeff Mullins and Jack Marin (future NBA stars) and a big size advantage with two 6'10" players (our biggest starter was 6'5"). But when the coach from Czechoslovakia was asked to make his pick, he chose UCLA. The others asked him why, and he said, "Is team." He meant that, while Duke had some great individuals and superior size, we simply—yet success-fully—played together as a team.

We were a group of athletes who had blended together well during the 1963 season even though we lost nine games. We might have been unimpressive physically, but we knew Coach Wooden's system inside out and played instinctively as a unit. Coach knew we could be very good.

Our secret weapon on that 1964 team was the 2-2-1

zone press. Coach Wooden has said that our individual skills fit the needs of the five different spots in the press just about as well as they could be filled.

Fred Slaughter, at 6'5" and 230 pounds, was big and broad and forced the in-bound pass to the left side of the floor, right into the strength of the left-handed Goodrich. Gail shut off the sideline, allowing Slaughter to come over for the double team.

Hazzard, long armed, aggressive, and quick handed, was behind Goodrich and ready to stop the drive or pick off any passes in his area. Hirsch, also left-handed, moved with his strong side right into the heart of the opponents' target area, the middle of the court.

Because of my background in tennis and volleyball, the number five spot was a natural for me. Anticipation of length-of-court passes was necessary, as well as quickness and jumping ability to hold off any fast-break attempts until my retreating teammates could catch up and get into our regular defense. I was like a safety in football, our last line of defense.

The purpose of the press was to make up for our size disadvantage. By pressing, we could take advantage of our quickness and conditioning to force our opponents to pick up the tempo of the game. Until the 1964 season, every team in our conference would walk the ball up the floor.

I don't think the coaches had any idea the press would be as successful as it was. In every game that season we had a scoring spurt triggered by our scrappy, full-court defense. Our opponents would have a lapse of a minute or two, and we would quickly run off 8, 10, or up to 18 unanswered points. After this blitz, in effect, the game would be over.

Things broke well for us all season long. In addition to an injury-free season, one of Coach Wooden's biggest surprises was the play of the two sophomores off the bench—Washington and McIntosh. As freshmen, they had not been overly impressive, so Coach wasn't expecting too much from them. But all season long Kenny and Doug made major contributions, none bigger than in the Final Four championship game against Duke, when they played most of the game and combined for 34 points.

Back in the sixties, to get into the NCAA tournament, you had to win your conference. There were no "at large" teams. We were able to do that in 1964 by going 15-0 against some talented conference teams.

At the end of league play, we were 26-0. Next up was the NCAA tournament, and two tough West Coast teams—the University of Seattle and the University of San Francisco—were licking their chops, ready to devour the little bitty Bruins.

The regionals were played in Corvallis, Oregon, and the University of Seattle was our first hurdle. They were big and good. It was a tough game. We led by 10 at the half, 49-39, but fell behind 75-73 with a little under eight minutes to play. With five minutes left, we were up 81-80, and we held that 1-point lead until the final forty-one

Walt Hazzard was an uncanny ball handler. When he had the ball, you needed to be watching because he would get the ball to you one way or the other—either into your waiting hands or bouncing off your chest if you weren't paying attention. Walt grew up in the East and played high school ball at Overbrook in Philadelphia—home of a great basketball tradition that produced Wilt Chamberlain, Wayne Hightower, Wally Jones, and others.

seconds. Then we ran off 7 in a row and finally won 95-90. Hazzard and Goodrich had 26 and 19 points respectively, and future NBA star John Tresvant led Seattle with 20 points.

Once again our physical stamina had paid off. Walt Hazzard remembers the role conditioning played all season in our success: "We never played against a team that was in better condition than we were. We would stand in our huddle during time-outs while the other teams ran to the bench and sat down."

Every team we faced had a size advantage on us, and even though we were undefeated, we were usually considered the underdog.

The University of San Francisco was next, the following day. They had three future pros who started: Ollie Johnson (6'8"), Erwin Mueller (6'8"), and Joe Ellis (6'6").

We were down by 13 points in the first half, but we hung in there waiting for our "run." At the start of the second half, we outscored USF 17-8 and led 45-44 with fourteen minutes to go. The Dons' last lead was at 48-47. With Hazzard leading the troops with 23 points, we held them off 76-72.

Now we were on the way to "the Big Show" in Kansas City—the Final Four. Our first-round draw was Kansas State, a team we had played in our third game of the season and beaten 78-75. Our coaches were concerned that we might let down, as we had knocked off the Wildcats earlier. Plus, Kansas State was flying high with a thirteen-game win streak.

The Wildcats played well. Their coach, Tex Winters, had them well prepared for us, and with seven minutes to go, they were up 75-70. At that point our cheerleaders, delayed by travel difficulties, rushed into the arena and brought some much-needed moral support. We promptly ran off 11 points in a row and held off K State 90-84. On to the championship game!

The next night it was David versus Goliath again. The little Bruins, undefeated and unappreciated, against the mighty Blue Devils of Duke—with their two 6'10" giants—colossal and confident.

For the first eight minutes it was give and take, with Duke leading 30-27. But the knockout punch was quick and decisive. We ran off 16 consecutive points to lead 43-30. For all intents and purposes, the game was over. We finished it 98-83, and the first national championship for John Wooden and the UCLA Bruins was in the books.

That first title in 1964 was to become the cornerstone in UCLA's dynasty. The second crown, taken during my senior year, further solidified the Bruins's great basketball future.

Coach Wooden has said that those two championships are what attracted the attention of a young man in New York.

John Wooden:

"We wouldn't have gotten him [Lew Alcindor] if

we hadn't won in 1964 and 1965. His high school coach called me after we won the title in '65 and told me they had watched the championship. Alcindor said, after watching the Bruins, that UCLA was one of five schools he would visit before deciding what college to go to."

Coach Wooden had a policy of not contacting out-of-state prospects, but he was willing to follow up if an out-of-state prospect contacted him, and this one was definitely worth contacting. Coaches Wooden and Norman flew to New York City and met with Mr. and Mrs. Alcindor. It was a favorable meeting, and Kareem moved west to join the Bruins.

A tall young redhead from San Diego, Bill Walton also loved the way those championship teams played. That was how he wanted to play and UCLA was where he wanted to go.

Kareem and Walton were the heart and soul of an incredible run of championships—a record that will probably never be matched in any sport.

But it all started in 1964 with an unlikely group of guys who were "just too short."

The Master's Touch

3

UCLA is recognized as having one of the premier basketball programs in the United States. But it would not have attained its reputation for excellence if it were not for one man: John Robert Wooden.

Coach Wooden is often called the Wizard of Westwood, a nickname he dislikes. But his commitment to his players, as well as his "team" philosophy, resulted in his now having more NCAA championships than any coach in college basketball history. Coach Wooden taught his players to work as a team, and then he let them play.

In his forty years as a head coach (twenty-seven years at UCLA), Coach Wooden's teams won 885 games and lost 203. That's an astounding .813 winning percentage!

From 1964 to 1975, the Bruins won ten national championships in twelve years. This included an amazing seven in a row.

Coach Wooden's record at UCLA included 620 wins, nineteen conference titles, an eighty-eight-game winning streak, and four undefeated seasons. He is the only person inducted into the Basketball Hall of Fame as both a coach and a player. I don't think these records will ever be seriously challenged.

Even more important than Wooden's records, though, is the indelible impression he left on the approximately 350 players he coached at UCLA. A master motivator, he did his task in a way that left these players prepared for a lot more than basketball. He prepared his players for life.

A teacher as well as a coach, Coach would methodically lay out the concept he was trying to teach. Once players understood the big picture, he would break it down into its parts. He believed that learning involved explanation, demonstration, correction, and repetition, repetition, and more repetition.

Wooden loved practices. The gymnasium was his classroom. He believed that games tested players on what they had learned in practice. He prepared so thoroughly—with practices planned down to the smallest detail—because he believed that "failing to prepare was preparing to fail."

Coach Wooden's recruiting methods were a bit unor-

That's me, number 53, setting a screen for the high-scoring Gail Goodrich. Gail was so small (just 5'11" and 130 pounds as a high school junior) that many colleges chose not to recruit him. His father had been captain of the basketball team at USC, but the Trojans didn't think Gail was a "chip off the old block" until his senior season, when Gail had already chosen UCLA. Gail scored 42 points in the 1965 NCAA championship game.

thodox by current standards. He actively sought players in southern California, but his policy was never to contact players outside that area. "I didn't feel it was necessary," he said. "If you do well, you are going to get a wealth of material from other parts of the country. You're going to attract them because success breeds success.

"I never wanted to *talk* a player into coming to UCLA. I wanted players who *wanted* to come to UCLA."

No doubt, Coach Wooden's greatest recruit was a 7'2" young man "who wanted to come to UCLA" from New York City. His name was Lew Alcindor. Kareem holds a special place in Wooden's memory as the most valuable player ever to play at UCLA.

John Wooden:

"To me he is the most valuable player that I ever had. Maybe Walton was a better center, if you wanted to grade every fundamental skill of the game on a one-to-ten basis and then add them all up. I think Walton would be considered as fine a center as has ever played, but he was still not as valuable as Kareem, because Kareem forced the other team to change both offensively and defensively. He was also an extremely unselfish player, and that helps the other players get better control over their game."

Wooden believes Kareem's height was only one factor

in his greatness. "He was amazing, not just because of his size but because of his agility and composure," he says. "He took more of a beating than most people realize. He hardly ever lost his composure the years that I had him. He kept his emotions under pretty good control all the time."

Jay Carty, a former Oregon State basketball player who wanted to stay involved in the game and was working on his doctorate, made a valuable contribution as an unpaid coach to help prepare Kareem.

John Wooden:

"I needed someone strong to work against Kareem, because I had no one of any particular size [Jay is 6'8"], and he worked with Kareem as a freshman.

"I talked to Kareem and told him, `The biggest difference you're going to find in the freshman and varsity teams is the roughness of the game, and you'll find the same thing when you leave college and go to the pros. You're going to find a tremendous difference in the physical aspect of the game, but I want you to learn to take it and keep your temper. Jay's not going to do anything to hurt you, but I want him to bump you around.'

"Jay did that daily, and I think he had a lot to do with Kareem's development."

Coach Wooden always felt the team was more important than any one player. Sidney Wicks was a perfect example.

John Wooden:

"Wicks was very bright. I never had a player with more physical ability to play the forward position than Sidney Wicks. He had height, speed, and was a fine competitor.

"In clutch situations, when we had to have the free throw, I would rather have had Sidney on the line than almost any other player we had—even though he wasn't the best free-throw shooter. In the clutch, he would get the rebound for you. He would block the shot or make the play we needed.

"As a sophomore he got mad because he didn't start. I started Lynn Shackleford and Curtis Rowe instead. Sidney would say to me, `But coach, you know I'm better than they are,' and I would say, `Yes I know it, you know it, and everybody knows it, but it's a shame you're letting them beat you out.'

"He was a one-on-one player, and I just didn't like that. I don't think he was a selfish individual. He just played that way, so sitting on the bench as a

Kareem Abdul-Jabbar (Lew Alcindor during his college years) was such a force that he altered the way college basketball was played. During his tenure at UCLA, the Bruins won three consecutive NCAA championships and lost only two games. While a college player, a joke circulated that the meaning of the letters NCAA was "No Chance Against Alcindor."

sophomore made him a better player his last two years and later as a pro."

In John Wooden's eyes, it was more important that players fill their role on the team rather than exhibit outstanding one-on-one skills. The team always came first.

Coach Wooden recalled this story about Wicks and Steve Patterson and their political convictions in the '60s.

Wicks and Patterson wanted to skip practice one day so they could protest the Vietnam War along with other students. The coach always taught his players to stand up for their convictions, but missing practice was not an option. Wooden had his convictions, too, and one was that no player who was physically able should ever miss practice. Wicks and Patterson were told that if they missed practice, it would be the end of their careers at UCLA. They stayed!

The master's touch left its greatest mark, perhaps, on one of Wooden's most challenging pupils: Bill Walton. Walton attributes much of his success as a player and as a person to Coach Wooden, and he relishes the opportunity to reminisce about his days at UCLA.

Bill Walton:

"The first basketball game I ever saw on television as a kid was the 1965 UCLA national champi-onship game against Michigan. My family didn't have a television set, so I watched it at a friend's house in San Diego. Michigan had great players like Cazzie Russell and Bill Buntin—muscular studs—and here were all these skinny, scrawny guys from southern California who were killing them with teamwork and fundamentals. The Bruins just ran circles around them. That was the game when Gail Goodrich had 42 points in the finals, and UCLA won because of its quickness, teamwork, passing, and perfect execution of fundamentals.

"That was me, just a skinny little kid, and I told myself, `That's what I want to do.'

"After I saw them play, I modeled my whole game after the UCLA team; I was in love with UCLA basketball. Later, when I was playing for UCLA as a junior, breaking Goodrich's scoring record in the NCAA finals was really special to me.

"UCLA was the first school that contacted me. I got a letter from Denny Crum [UCLA Assistant Coach] when I was a sophomore in high school, encouraging me to take the right academic courses to get in. I was so excited about that letter. I told my mother from the first day I got it that I was going to UCLA. Academics were never a problem. My dad was into music and literature, and my mom's a librarian, and they had always emphasized the importance of education and made sure I kept my grades up.

"I told Coach Crum every day that I wanted to come to UCLA, but they still recruited me harder and more professionally than anybody else.

"I was one of the few high school players that Wooden ever came to see play, and he came to our house for dinner. My parents had gone through this whole recruiting game with my older brother, Bruce, who had ended up going to UCLA to play football as a defensive tackle. So they insisted that all the coaches who wanted to recruit me have dinner at our house.

"When Wooden came to the house we had a big meal. He tells a funny story about how much food we used to eat. He says my mom brought a *huge* platter of food in—and that was just for Bruce!

"Every other school that was recruiting me promised me everything under the sun. Some would say, `We're going to build the whole basketball program around you, Bill. You're going to set every record. You're going to score every time you touch the ball.'

"Coach Wooden was different. He said, `I know that they're promising you everything, but I'm not even going to promise you're going to make our team. But I will promise you that if you come to UCLA and you work hard, you'll get a terrific education that will last you the rest of your life. And if you do make our team, there will be other really good players on the team with you.'"

What a powerful statement—particularly in light of college recruiting practices today and the depths to which some have sunk.

Bill Walton:

"He [Wooden] set such a standard of excellence that if you were a basketball player and you wanted to prove yourself, you just had to go to UCLA.

"The first game I saw at UCLA was Kareem's last. I was overwhelmed by the experience. I was fifteen or sixteen, and when the team came out of the locker room, the band struck up, and the cheerleaders and the crowd went crazy. It was the finals of the western regionals against Santa Clara, and the Bruins just killed them. I said to myself, `Yeah, that's for me.' That's what I wanted to do, so there was never any question in my mind where I was going to school.

"Denny Crum called me every Monday night for three years, and he always had a new story about what was going on with the team. He would have Coach Wooden get on the phone and say hello, and then he would arrange for me to see some of the other top players they were recruiting—like Greg Lee and Keith [Jamaal] Wilkes.

"I can remember sitting with John Wooden and Denny Crum, watching Greg Lee play, and Greg scored 35 points. He was awesome. And then I went and saw Wilkes play, and he was terrific."

Walton never regretted his decision to play for Coach Wooden.

Bill Walton:

"John Wooden was at his peak as a coach when I played for him. Because he had so many great players before I got there, I'm sure he was better than before, because of his experience with all of them.

"Coach Wooden had a bigger influence on me than anyone else in my life—outside of my mother and father. When I got to UCLA, he took the role of my parents.

"I didn't just spend practice time with Coach Wooden. I spent more time in his office than any other player. I would go see him every morning, asking him questions like, `How come I don't get to shoot more?' or `How come you have me playing this stupid high-post offense?' I didn't realize until afterwards the things he was teaching me. He had a demanding level of excellence, but he was never mean; he was always positive.

"The players didn't really believe and accept the lessons Coach Wooden was teaching until they left UCLA. When life comes apart, the stuff that Coach Wooden teaches you helps you pull it back together."

Like so many of us who played at UCLA, Walton has remained very loyal to Bruin basketball since he left the university.

Bill Walton:

"I used to help recruit, and whenever I was playing in Portland, I would try to catch the games. I am a Bruin; I am a real proud Bruin.

"I've been part of some great basketball teams. I feel I'm part of the two greatest basketball families there are—the UCLA Bruins and the Boston Celtics.

"You can see the impact Wooden has had on his players' lives in their eyes. You can also see it in their level of success. It's amazing. When you look back, there are really only about 350 guys who can say they played for him. You see them everywhere; they are doing all different kinds of things. John Wooden had the ability to take people and make them better performers in whatever it was they chose to do.

"The things I learned from John Wooden I apply to every area of my life. When I had to learn to overcome my speech impediment—stuttering—somebody gave me some basic keys. But the thing that helped me apply them was the lessons I learned from Wooden. He had this gift—helping people learn how to learn."

Wooden speaks highly of Walton, but as with other players, he had a balanced view of him from the first time he heard of him. Denny Crum had seen Bill play and had raved about him. Wooden actually scolded Denny for his high praise of Bill. Later, when the coach finally saw Walton play, Crum asked him, "Well what do you think?" Wooden replied, "Well he *is* pretty good." That was high praise coming from him!

Bill still calls Coach Wooden on a regular basis. As student and teacher, they take turns encouraging one another.

Current UCLA coach Jim Harrick respects Wooden so much that in his office in the athletic department he keeps an area that honors Wooden, with a commemorative

ASUCLA

Sidney Wicks had an outstanding career at UCLA. In his three years, the Bruins won three NCAA championships and lost only four games. Coach Wooden called Sidney the consummate power forward. He was twice a first-team All-American.

plate and a glass "Pyramid of Success" listing the values Wooden tried to instill in his players.

Coach Wooden has expressed his support for the job done by Coach Harrick, too, and the way the 1995 Bruins played. He thinks the players on the 1995 squad would have fit well into the championship teams of earlier years.

John Wooden:

"I thought the 1995 team had tenacity and that they were unselfish both on offense and defense. I was glad for Jim [Harrick], for reasons a lot of people might have overlooked. He has been a teacher in junior high and high school, and he's taught other subjects besides physical education. He served an apprenticeship at Utah State. He was an assistant coach to Gary Cunningham for two years and coached at Pepperdine. He's paid his dues.

"I like the 1995 players. They played their roles extremely well. The O'Bannons are nice fellows. George Zidek is a fine person and an outstanding student. I was always partial to little Tyus Edney; he has great court vision, and he has been a spark plug since he started playing on a regular basis. Toby Bailey and J. R. Henderson are also fine ballplayers."

So much goes into winning a championship, and two of the most important factors—according to Wooden—are talent and luck. "No one wins without talent," he says. "You need that, and somewhere along the way you need a little luck."

Although Wooden pays tribute to the talented players that Harrick has, and those he had over the years, he still believes that character is the basis of team basketball.

"I think character, more than talent, will enable you to come through in difficult situations. But you have to have talent too," he adds.

It's amazing to think of how college basketball has changed since Coach Wooden left coaching. He never made more than $32,500 as a coach—$40,000 total. He didn't have any big endorsement contracts or do television commercials or drive a fancy car. Today, that same position at UCLA pays many times what their greatest basketball coach ever made!

Coach Wooden had offers to coach at other schools, and he could have made more money—particularly in the NBA—but he always remained loyal to UCLA.

Jerry West, former college and pro basketball star with the Lakers, has said, "Wooden's desire hasn't been to be a wealthy man. If that had been the case, he could have been extremely wealthy. I think the tip-off on John is when you hear him speak. He has a message. This man really believes what he says."

Wooden remains humble about all the honor and glory

he has received. "A lot of things had to fall in place for us to win," he has said. "We had wonderful youngsters, and I was at a great university. So many things went our way."

For Coach Wooden, the most important things in life have nothing to do with wealth, but with teaching young players about a success that is independent of money—things that can help a person succeed in basketball *and* in life.

John Wooden is that rare, gifted person, a master teacher who had the ability to affect his students far beyond the years they were in his classroom.

The Incredible Run

4

After the 1964 championship, the Bruins started the 1965 season in a humbling way. We lost—badly—our first game against Illinois 110-83.

As Coach Wooden remembers it, Illinois really took the team apart, and it brought us to our senses.

There was more to it than that, though. We were no longer the unknown underdogs. Every team was gunning for us because we were the defending national champs. Our style of play was no longer a secret.

Gail Goodrich and I were named cocaptains. Fred Goss, Edgar Lacey, and Doug McIntosh replaced Hazzard, Hirsch, and Slaughter in our lineup. Coach Wooden was impressed with these replacements and how they rose to the challenge.

"Freddie Goss added more than what he gave in play because of his work ethic," said Wooden. "And Mike Lynn came in and did a good job." Remember, Coach Wooden never says much about an individual player's performance, so that was high praise.

Lacey, who had been on *Parade* magazine's High School All-America Team with a tall sophomore named Lew Alcindor, also played well.

Gail Goodrich had an amazing season. Now that Walt Hazzard had left for the NBA, Gail was both our playmaker and leading scorer—averaging 24 points per game, which is still a UCLA record for guards. I averaged half that many points and continued to enjoy my role as the back man in our press.

Our record in 1965 was 28-2. Wooden was proud of us because he felt we reached our maximum potential as a team. Goodrich scored 42 points in the NCAA championship game against an outstanding Michigan team; we beat them 91-80. Gail didn't win the tournament's Most Valuable Player award because (former U.S. Senator) Bill Bradley scored 58 points when Princeton beat Wichita State in the consolation game. Bradley got the MVP award. We got the championship trophy!

What made the 1965 title so crucial to UCLA's dynasty was not just the players on the court but also two youngsters watching on their television sets: Kareem Abdul-Jabbar and Bill Walton. Bill was just in junior high, but Kareem was the most sought-after high school senior in America.

Wooden is sure that Kareem was impressed when he saw UCLA become only the fifth school in NCAA history to win back-to-back titles in 1965. There were other factors that led to UCLA winning the recruiting battle for the big man, but the biggest, according to Wooden, was the completion of UCLA's sparkling new arena, Pauley Pavilion.

John Wooden:

"The reason I wanted Kareem to visit UCLA last was to show him Pauley Pavilion and how beautiful it was. I wanted to let him know that his first college game would be played to dedicate the building."

His strategy worked. After Kareem saw the campus and Pauley Pavilion, he called Coach Wooden and committed himself to UCLA.

The championships our team had won had definitely helped change things at UCLA. The once-poor athletic department was now able to afford recruiting trips. How the basketball program got on its feet is a story in itself.

Jerry Norman:

"We didn't have any money for recruiting, so I

came up with the idea of a freshmen-against-the-varsity game. [These were the days when freshmen were prevented by NCAA rules from playing on varsity teams.] Everybody had to pay to get in—even the coaches.

"The first year, we had the game in the old UCLA gym. We got the building and grounds guys to put up one side of the bleachers at no charge. Those seats sold for two dollars; everyone else had to stand. We made $3,000, which was a lot of money in 1962.

"The next year, we moved the game to Santa Monica's gym to seat more people."

UCLA Athletic Director J. D. Morgan knew a successful promotion when he saw it, so in the fall of 1965, when Kareem came in as a freshman, he asked Norman if the athletic department could run the fund-raising basketball game. In exchange, he would give the basketball program any funds they wanted for recruiting.

Because Pauley Pavilion seats 12,819, Morgan knew the athletic department was going to make thousands of dollars, because so many people wanted to see Kareem play his first game as a freshman.

Eventually Norman went out on recruiting trips all over the state of California, but he didn't do much travel to other states. "If we were able to recruit the top two or three senior high school basketball players in our state,

Keith Wilkes was so proficient in such an effortless manner, he became known as "Smooth as Silk" Wilkes. Keith was a perfect compliment to his dominating teammate Bill Walton. He became an NBA star for the L.A. Lakers for eight years.

then I felt we didn't need that many players from outside the state, and the only way we would go after someone out of state is if they were really great," said Norman.

After bringing home the championship for the second year in a row in 1965, UCLA had won over the prospect that would matter the most. Kareem was a force that would permanently change the college game.

If the NCAA had let freshmen play when Kareem came to UCLA, the Bruins probably would have had an even longer string of titles. In the fall of 1965, the fresh-man team—led by Abdul-Jabbar, Lucius Allen, and Lynn Shackelford—beat the varsity team 75-60. "You always have to have one or two really outstanding players to win a national title, and in the 1965-1966 season the varsity team didn't have them," said Assistant Coach Norman. UCLA surrendered the championship crown quietly. They finished the season 18-8, taking second place in confer-ence play and missing the NCAA tournament for the first time in five years.

But 1967 would be different. Now Kareem and his talented teammates were sophomores and ready to join the varsity. No center has ever dominated a game like Kareem would. He had a great variety of short-range shots and slam dunks. In his first year, he set the school record for points in a game with 56. Later that year, when the Bruins played Washington State, he broke his own record with 61 points.

Assistant Coach Jerry Norman recalls how teams re-sorted to desperate measures to try to beat UCLA.

Jerry Norman:

"When Abdul-Jabbar was a sophomore, we were playing Oregon. They decided to hold the ball. [This was before the forty-five-second shot clock in college basketball.] At halftime it was 18 to 14, with UCLA ahead. There were ten thousand people who wanted to see Kareem play, but we decided to hold the ball ourselves in the second half. At the end of the game we (facetiously) told the press that we thought Oregon *wanted* us to hold the ball."

"There were no thoughts of a college basketball dynasty in my mind until the Bruins got Kareem," said Norman.

It wasn't just having one great player, though. UCLA had a *team* of good players. They had a strong shooter in Lynn Shackelford, a savvy team leader in Mike Warren (who became a television star on the show *Hill Street Blues)*, and a great defensive player in Kenny Heitz.

The first of seven championships in a row was won in 1967, 79-64 against Dayton.

The NCAA changed the rules after Kareem's sophomore year and outlawed dunking, but Coach Wooden is convinced the change made Kareem a better all-around basketball player.

In Kareem's three varsity seasons, UCLA went 30-0, 29-1, and 29-1. In fact, there was only one constant foe in those years who even challenged UCLA, and that was

Houston and their multitalented star, 6'9" Elvin Hayes. The "Big E," as he was called, not only played tough in the paint but could shoot like a guard.

In their first meeting in the semifinals of the 1967 Final Four, Hayes outscored Abdul-Jabbar 25-19 and outrebounded him 24-20. But UCLA was more than its star center's individual stats, and the Bruins won convincingly, 73-58.

The rivalry between Abdul-Jabbar and Hayes became like a basketball boxing match. In 1968 the two players put college basketball on the mind of every American sports fan with the UCLA-Houston game, held at the Houston Astrodome in front of 52,693. It was the largest crowd to see a college basketball game up to that time.

The game was nationally televised and laid the foundation for the college game's ensuing popularity. Now fifty million people watch the NCAA finals in prime time.

Houston won round number two by just 2 points, 71-69, on the strength of Hayes's 39 points and 15 rebounds. This stopped UCLA's winning streak at forty-seven games. Kareem, playing with a badly bruised eye, still managed to score 18 points and get 12 rebounds. Their defeat made the Bruins angry. Now they had something to prove.

In the 1968 NCAA semifinals, with a healthy Kareem and a double-team defense on Hayes (a diamond and one),

UCLA led 53-31 at halftime. The Bruins later built a 44-point lead, and it was all over but for the final margin.

Lynn Shackelford followed Elvin Hayes wherever he went in that defensive set. Elvin also had to contend with an angry Kareem, whom Hayes had told the media was "overrated." The "Big E" scored only 10 points.

The Bruins finished with a 101-69 victory. UCLA went on to its fourth NCAA championship in five years, beating North Carolina the following day by 23 points, 78-55. That set a record for the biggest margin of victory in a title game. No one questioned the greatness of the 1968 team and its place in college basketball history.

Even with the dunk shot outlawed, Kareem averaged 26 points per game as a junior, leading a balanced attack with all starters in double figures—Lucius Allen averaged 15 ponts; Mike Warren, 12; Lynn Shackelford, 10; and Mike Lynn, 10.

In the 1969 season, the biggest challenge for UCLA was to develop guards who could pass the ball to seniors Kareem and Shackelford, as well as feed two outstanding sophomore forwards, Curtis Rowe and Sidney Wicks.

The Bruins had lost a potential recruit, Paul Westphal, who decided to go to USC instead of UCLA. This gave Norman the green light to go after John Vallely, who became known as the Money Man for his play in big games. The Bruins wouldn't have recruited him at all if they had gotten Westphal.

Ironically, USC with Westphal beat UCLA 46-44 in

the 1969 season, which was the first time the Bruins lost in Pauley Pavilion during the Alcindor years.

The only other time the Bruins came close to losing that year was in the NCAA semifinals, when they beat Drake by only 3 points, 85-82. In that game, Vallely outscored Kareem 29-25.

The following day the Bruins became the first team in NCAA history to win three straight titles when they beat Purdue and their high-scoring guard, Rick Mount, 92-72. Kenny Heitz, the defensive specialist, did a great job guarding Mount.

Abdul-Jabbar won three straight Most Outstanding Player awards in the NCAA tournament and went on to a brilliant career in the NBA as the league's all-time leading scorer. There was a joke that during his years at UCLA, the letters NCAA meant "No Chance Against Alcindor."

In 1970 UCLA won the championship again, this time led by Sidney Wicks, a man with great one-on-one skills and one of the best forwards to ever play at UCLA.

The championship game in 1970 was another classic, pitting the Bruins against the Jacksonville Dolphins. The Dolphins had two seven-footers on the front line: the great Artis Gilmore, and Pembroke Burrows III. The Dolphins also had a fine shooting guard named Rex Morgan.

Jacksonville took a 14-6 early lead over the Bruins, but then a defensive innovation to stop Gilmore started working. UCLA used a defensive trap that sagged in on Gilmore. Wicks acted as the final line of defense against

In his own way, the towering redhead Bill Walton was as dominant at the center position as Kareem Abdul-Jabbar. The Bruins won NCAA titles during Bill's reign and were without a loss those two years. To this day Bill is very close to Coach Wooden, but when he was a player, he often questioned the coach's strategy and style. Bill still holds the record for most points scored in an NCAA final—44— and that was before 3-point baskets.

Gilmore and blocked five of his shots. The Bruins won 80-69 for their fourth NCAA championship in a row.

The season was rewarding for the squad because they proved they could win the championship—even without Abdul-Jabbar.

In 1971, with Wicks, Rowe, Steve Patterson, and Henry Bibby back, the team just got better. And on the horizon was an even brighter future with the most talked about freshman team on campus since the group that included Abdul-Jabbar. Bill Walton, Keith (Jamaal) Wilkes, and Greg Lee were being groomed to carry on the tradition.

The 1971 Bruins went 29-1, with an 89-82 loss to Notre Dame being the last defeat they would suffer for three years. The mark of this Bruin team was coming from behind to win close games. UCLA won seven games by 5 points or less.

In the west regionals they trailed Jerry Tarkanian's Cal State Long Beach team by 11 points before coming back to win 57-55.

In the NCAA championship game they beat Villanova 68-62. Steve Patterson, the often-overlooked center, was the game's hero, scoring 29 points as the Bruins claimed their fifth title in a row.

In 1972 the media nicknamed the UCLA basketball team The Walton Gang. The 6'11" redheaded center from San Diego would dominate college basketball for the next three years.

In his first season, Walton was simply amazing. He tied Abdul-Jabbar's record for most rebounds in a season with 466. And he averaged 21 points a game. It wasn't just Walton, though, because this outstanding team had balanced scoring and diversity of talent with other great players in Keith (Jamaal) Wilkes, Greg Lee, and Henry Bibby, all of whom scored in double figures.

With Walton leading the way, the Bruins scored 100 points in their first seven games. They went undefeated at 30-0, and only one team—Oregon State—came close to beating UCLA during the regular season, a 78-72 Bruin victory.

Interestingly enough, Denny Crum, who had recruited Bill Walton to come to UCLA, was now coaching Louisville. Bill, never missing an opportunity, kidded Crum just before UCLA beat the Cardinals that year in the NCAA semifinals. Walton had 33 points against his former mentor's new team.

UCLA won the national championship, their sixth in a row, by beating Florida State 81-76 at the Los Angeles Sports Arena.

The 1972 Bruins set an NCAA record that still stands, defeating their opponents by an average of 30 points per game.

In Walton's junior year, the 1973 team was again 30-0 and undefeated for the season, which made the Bruins the only team in college basketball history to post four undefeated seasons and the only team to go undefeated back-to-back.

The 1973 team set many records, including the surpassing of the University of San Francisco's record of sixty straight wins (during the era of the great Bill Russell). By the end of the year their consecutive streak stood at seventy-five, and Walton set a school record for rebounds in a season with 506. This record is still in the books too.

Walton had his best game ever in the 1973 NCAA championship game. He was everywhere, making twenty-one of twenty-two shots from the floor and scoring 44 points. Both of these are still records for an NCAA title game. The Bruins beat Memphis State in the championship game, 87-66. The Memphis State coach, Gene Bartow, would replace Wooden as UCLA coach three years later.

Halfway through the 1974 season, the winning streak stood at eighty-eight games. Looking back, Coach Wooden says he felt that after all this success Walton and his teammates had become a little complacent. Bill says to this day he wishes he had some of those days and games back from the '73-'74 season to play again.

The end of the winning streak for UCLA started when they lost an 11-point lead over Notre Dame in South Bend in the last three minutes. The Fighting Irish squeezed out a 71-70 win.

In the 1974 NCAA semifinals, UCLA faced North Carolina State. They had beaten the Wolfpack in the

The numbers worn by Kareem Abdul-Jabbar and Bill Walton were retired at a special ceremony in 1990. Coach Wooden didn't play at UCLA, so no jersey number could be retired for him. But in the hearts of Bruin fans, he'll always be number one.

regular season by 18 points. North Carolina State over-
came an 11-point UCLA lead to tie the game and send it
into overtime. After the first overtime, the teams were still
tied. In the second overtime period, UCLA jumped out to
a 7-point lead, but the Wolfpack came back again and won
the game 80-77. The great David Thompson, North Carolina State's best player, led the Wolfpack to the thrilling
victory with 28 points.

Walton still calls this loss the biggest disappointment
of his basketball career. The Bruins's record of thirty-eight
straight NCAA tournament wins ended. It was an incredible run, and even with the disappointing loss, UCLA had
one more championship in them before the drought.

In the 1974-75 season, some new players brought a
revival spirit to the team. The Walton Gang had graduated,
and these new players wanted to taste UCLA-style success. Only one senior, Dave Meyers, took an aggressive
leadership role. Meyers averaged more than 18 points per
game and was strongly supported by two great sophomores, Richard Washington and Marques Johnson. Andre
McCarter, a junior, assumed the playmaker role.

A particular favorite of Coach Wooden's that year was
Marques Johnson (who is now the radio announcer for the
Bruins). Wooden had a dilemma: He wanted Johnson to
play, but over the summer Johnson had contracted hepatitis and was under doctor's orders to be played sparingly.

Johnson still averaged in double figures, but as
Wooden remembers it, "The doctors had said, `Don't let

him get too tired.' Now he was over the hepatitis and feeling pretty good, but I was still following the doctor's orders. He was upset with me that I wouldn't let him play more during the regular season."

Finally, during the NCAA tournament, Wooden was given the green light by the doctors to play Johnson freely, and the youngster responded. In the west regional game against Arizona State, Johnson scored 35 points to lead UCLA to an 89-75 victory. "Marques had the best vertical jump of any player I ever had," Wooden says. "If he got the ball off the board, no one was going to stop him as a rebounder or scorer. He would take somebody with him on each arm because he had that great jumping ability. There was no doubt in my mind that he was going to go down in history as one of the best players we ever had at UCLA."

In the Final Four in 1975, UCLA played one of the toughest games in its history. They barely defeated Louisville 75-74 in overtime in the semifinals. Coach Wooden showed the strain of the pressure-packed game. The stress of coaching was starting to affect his health. He hadn't slept well for the last couple of weeks. He had turned down the opportunity to coach the 1976 U.S. Olympic team on the advice of his doctor.

Before the championship game, Wooden, 64, announced that he was going to retire—not because he wanted to but because he had to.

UCLA played a great final game against Kentucky.

Richard Washington led the scoring with 28 points. Meyers, who was also in his last game, had 24.

And Wooden walked away from UCLA with ten NCAA titles in twelve years. It is a record for the ages.

College basketball has changed dramatically since John Wooden retired. But I believe UCLA's incredible run of championships under the master's leadership will stand the test of time.

The Long Drought

5

How does a team go from winning seven consecutive NCAA championships and ten titles in twelve years to not winning another one for twenty years? It took UCLA six coaches, two decades, and a lot of frustration to find out.

The Bruins weren't just accustomed to playing in the NCAA tournament, they were used to winning it. You didn't need a calendar to know when March Madness began. All you had to do was check the UCLA watch on your wrist! You know the UCLA watch? (Don't bother setting it. It always runs fast. Wind it up, and it's time for another championship!)

Then that UCLA watch broke. The stem snapped, the springs fell out, the gears went haywire, and the whole thing lay there on the floor in a heap. It didn't

tick again for twenty years. Call it a drought, even though that probably doesn't do it justice. After all, calling something that lasted twenty years a mere drought is like calling the Mojave Desert a sandbox.

Needless to say, it wasn't the best of times around Westwood. Until Jim Harrick's arrival, only one of the five coaches who followed Wooden and preceded Harrick lasted as long as four years.

Opposing teams were no longer in awe of UCLA. The Bruins's invincibility was now challenged rather than acknowledged.

In the '50s and early '60s, the Bruins were fortunate if they had a handful of fans following them on the road, even to regional tournament games. Now, after their many championships, they were followed by thousands. And these fans were eager to let the UCLA coaches know when they weren't pleased with the team's performance.

Their expectations were intense and totally unrealistic. The Bruins could go through the conference season undefeated, win the league championship, even go to the Final Four. But if they didn't win it all, in the eyes of their fans, they had failed.

And the irony is that the greatest of lessons are often learned from failure. Critics weren't going to allow the Bruins to fail (not win the NCAA championship) and then respond to their failure, as even their idol Coach Wooden had done.

The UCLA basketball program was the envy of every

ASUCLA

Mike Warren was one of Coach Wooden's all-time favorite point guards. A coach-on-the-floor type, he made very few mistakes. Mike went on to a very successful acting career in Hollywood.

basketball fan and coach around the country throughout the Wooden years. Because of the Bruins's unparalleled success, they were able to sign great players year in and year out. But when John Wooden retired, UCLA no longer had a clear edge in recruiting. The coaches who followed Wooden were quality men and had outstanding ability, but they were at the wrong place at the wrong time.

Every basketball program in the country would be proud to have coaches the quality of Gene Bartow, Gary Cunningham, Larry Brown, Larry Farmer, and Walt Hazzard. And the success they achieved would have been more than enough if they had not been walking in the shadow of a legend.

Bartow was the first coach to follow Wooden, and he faced constant comparison with him. The criticism began before his first game was even over, as the Bruins lost their opener by 20 points. Bartow had some great talent with Marques Johnson, Richard Washington, and Andre McCarter. But the Bruins lost to an outstanding Indiana team in the NCAA semifinals, which unleashed the wrath of many UCLA fans.

Bartow thought the comparisons with Wooden would go away after the first year, but they didn't, and his health was being affected by the pressure to win. He quit in 1977 and took a job as athletic director and basketball coach at the University of Alabama at Birmingham. His record was an exceptional 52-9, but Wooden's teams had lost only eight times in the previous five years.

The quiet and gentlemanly Gary Cunningham followed Gene Bartow. Gary had played for Coach Wooden and had been his assistant for ten years. His two-year record at UCLA was 50-8, which would have satisfied just about anyone, but it didn't play all that well in Westwood. In his first year, he lost twice to Notre Dame and again in the first round of the NCAA west regional against Sydney Moncrief and the Arkansas Razorbacks.

David Greenwood and Kiki Vandeweghe returned to lead the Bruins to the west regional finals in Cunningham's second year, but the Bruins lost to DePaul and Mark Aguirre, 95-94.

It just wasn't enough to have a winning percentage of .862, two conference championships, and two appearances in the west regional, so Gary stepped down.

Larry Brown was up next. He had played at the University of North Carolina in the early '60s and had been a teammate of Walt Hazzard's on the gold-medal-winning U.S. Olympic basketball team in 1964. He had also played in the ABA professionally and had coached in both the ABA and NBA for seven years—most recently for the Denver Nuggets.

Although UCLA finished fourth in the Pac-10 and was 17-9 going into the NCAA tournament, Coach Brown's first Bruin team beat Old Dominion, DePaul, Ohio State, Clemson, and Purdue in 1980 to get to the NCAA finals against Louisville. Future NBA star Kiki Vandeweghe was Brown's leader. After leading the Cardinals by 2 at the half, Louisville—behind Darrell Griffith's 23 points—came back to edge the Bruins 59-54 for the title. It would be the last UCLA appearance in the championship game until 1995.

In 1981 Brown led the Bruins to a 20-7 record, third place in the Pac-10, and another trip to the NCAA tournament. But in their first game UCLA was bounced by Brigham Young (Danny Ainge scored 37 points) 78-55, and Brown—tired of enduring the "disappointment" of UCLA followers—had had enough. He was off to the NBA again with the New Jersey Nets.

Larry Farmer was UCLA's fourth "post-Wooden" coach. Larry had played on three NCAA championship teams under Wooden, and he bled blue and gold. However, the season hadn't even started, and Farmer was already dealing with big problems. UCLA had been placed on two years' probation because of NCAA rule violations by an overzealous Bruin fan.

Larry lasted three seasons and had a 61-23 record as well as a .726 winning percentage. But he was also the object of much criticism. After a 17-11 record in 1984, the school's worst in twenty-four years, he was forced to hire two assistant coaches—Walt Hazzard and Jack Hirsch, two players from the first championship team back in 1964. Because of the pressure to bring in the two new guys, Farmer was awarded a two-year contract extension and the proverbial "vote of confidence." After thinking it over for four days, Larry decided this arrangement wasn't worth it and resigned.

Hazzard was signed as head coach within hours. As it turned out, he lasted longer than anyone before him in the post-Wooden era: four years.

The Bruins won the NIT in Walt's first year, won the Pac-10 in his third year, had a 77-47 overall record, and sent Reggie Miller and Pooh Richardson (among others) to the NBA. But the comparisons with Wooden continued.

During Walt's stay, several of the top southern California prep players had opted for the East Coast and more TV exposure. That was bad enough to Bruin fans, but the last straw came when a couple of UCLA players left UCLA to transfer to other local programs. "Coach Wooden never would have let that happen," was the wail, and Hazzard was on his way out.

Jim Harrick replaced Hazzard in 1988 after UCLA tried unsuccessfully to hire Jim Valvano, Mike Kryzewski, and Larry Brown—again. Harrick had spent the last nine years as Pepperdine's head coach, winning five conference titles. He had paid his dues, from high school coach at Morningside in Inglewood, California (nine years), to college assistant at Utah St. (four years) and UCLA (two years), to head coach at Pepperdine. Now he was offered the job he'd been waiting for—head coach at UCLA.

The Herrick era began with a fast break. He signed local star Don MacLean in his first month on the job.

Shortly thereafter he recruited Darrick Martin, Tracy Murray, and Mitchell Butler, all future NBA players.

Harrick was a fundamentals coach like John Wooden and an unabashed John Wooden disciple. Harrick always made a point of shaking Wooden's hand before games and often invoked Wooden's name and philosophies and adopted them as his own.

Just like his five predecessors, Coach Harrick had ample success at UCLA—good enough for any program in the country . . . except UCLA. Because he had not won the championship, he was subjected to ridicule and criticism. It was the usual stuff: He couldn't recruit, he couldn't relate to the players or the media, he was not outgoing, he was insecure, etc.

Even some former players, such as Bill Walton, were frustrated with Harrick's teams because they felt players didn't exemplify the classic unselfish style of Bruin team basketball.

Bill Walton:

"Prior to the 1995 season there were players who were not in condition to play good basketball. Also, I didn't like the way the players were playing—the selfishness and greediness they were showing.

"They weren't showing respect for opponents; they weren't showing respect for UCLA basketball and how important it is. Putting on a UCLA basketball uniform is a very special honor. You have to put it all on the line. You can't have the attitude of `It's okay to lose' if you are true to the UCLA uniform.

"I talked to Harrick about that this year because I didn't feel he was instilling the right spirit in the players. Later I apologized. Because I'm an intense guy, I tend to expect a lot."

Jim Harrick, though, was a survivor. Maybe it was his West Virginia upbringing that toughened him up. Maybe it was the years he spent as an assistant, waiting for his chance. Maybe it was the experience he got from his nine years as Pepperdine's head coach. Maybe Harrick just kept his eyes open and saw the fine UCLA coaches before him come and go.

Whatever the reason, there would be another championship banner hanging from the rafters at Pauley Pavilion, and the no-nonsense strategist with the soft West Virginian drawl would be the one who got it. The long drought was about to end.

A Championship Season

6

In the second game of the 1994-95 season, UCLA beat Kentucky 82-81 in the John Wooden Classic held at the Arrowhead Pond Arena in Anaheim, California. After the game, UCLA Chancellor Charles Young spoke to the team and told them he thought they had what it took to go all the way to the national championship. Was the chancellor just caught up in the excitement, or did he have prophetic insight?

I had watched all the other national championship teams, and I agreed with the chancellor: The 1995 Bruins were the closest in style and talent to those prior teams.

Few people knew how hard team members—led by Ed O'Bannon—were preparing themselves for 1994-95. One of the keys to UCLA's return to the top

of men's college basketball is the preseason training the team put in after the 112-102 loss to Tulsa in the 1994 NCAA tournament. Under the direction of UCLA strength coach Phil Frye, the Bruins began right away to improve themselves physically for 1995. The preseason conditioning work started with an old standby—running.

"Running is the base of all the conditioning work we do," said Frye. "Then we build on it with weight training."

Phil is a strong advocate of weight training for basketball players, which is still a controversial type of preparation among many coaches. Many believe basketball players shouldn't do any weight training at all. They feel it hurts a player's shot and quickness if he puts on too much muscle. They say the players get enough work on the court and that the best preparation is to work on basketball skills.

Frye believes that strength is necessary for all sports, and the only way to get the kind of strength necessary to get the job done is through weight lifting.

"I'm so fortunate that I have had coaches here at UCLA who have believed in and supported weight training and believe in conditioning," said Frye. Frye gives credit, too, to a cooperative attitude from players, in particular Ed O'Bannon.

Phil Frye:
"Ed bit into the strength-training program more than anyone on the entire team, and when some of

the other players saw what it was doing for him as a player, they got interested too. He was like a Pied Piper because the players followed his lead. He put on about ten pounds and got a lot stronger.

"In the preseason, Ed lifted weights for an hour and fifteen minutes a day, five days a week. He loved the feeling it gave him so much that he decided to lift weights even on game days. He would have lifted up to an hour before game time if I had let him, but we decided that a more sensible thing to do was to lift weights together four hours before the game.

"Ed was put on a program to increase his muscle size and strength, and like everyone else, he ran forty-five minutes to an hour, three to four times a week. This was in addition to the work he did on the basketball court, and he was lifting weights during the season three to four days a week."

Even after Ed lifted on game days, he oftentimes had good shooting games, so Frye doesn't buy the argument from traditionalists that working with weights will ruin a basketball player's shot. Ed continued his weight-training regimen from preseason to the day of the national title game. When Frye tried to discourage him from lifting on that day, O'Bannon told him, "No way, coach. We're going to do exactly what brought us here."

One of the big reasons the season got off to such a great start is that the players got behind Coach Harrick and gave him their full support. A tough task for all coaches is getting players to accept the team concept. In years past, some players were more interested in their individual performance than the team's success. That kind of attitude makes it extremely difficult for a coach to build a strong team. The 1995 Bruins rallied around Coach Harrick after he was criticized for the team's poor performance the year before.

The 1995 Bruins made a commitment to get in better shape. They started the season well tuned physically and got stronger as the season progressed. UCLA played with more hunger, more pride, and a greater sense of responsibility. They were a fun team to watch and so unselfish they passed the ball almost to a fault. Each player aggressively went after rebounds, and there was no bickering and dissension—as there had been in the past.

Preseason preparation was as important for the 1995 team as it was for the great Wooden teams. But they too needed what Wooden had dubbed "exams called games" to see if what they were doing in practice would work where it counted most.

The first exam came against unheralded Cal State Northridge, and the Bruins passed with flying colors. But that game was an open-book pop quiz compared to what was coming. In the first game of the inaugural John Wooden Classic, UCLA ran straight into the third-ranked

Reggie Miller is one of many outstanding basketball players who attended UCLA but never had the chance to "cut down the nets" after a national championship. Reggie played for the Bruins in the 1980s before beginning his pro career with the Indiana Pacers. He's known for his long-range 3-point bombs.

Kentucky Wildcats, coached by Rick Pitino. Actually, Pitino probably knew the Bruins, or at least one in particular, as well as anyone. It was Pitino who had been the featured speaker at Charles O'Bannon's high school basketball banquet, when the recruiting war for Charles was so intense it looked like a staff meeting at the Pentagon.

Anyway, the Bruins fell behind the hot-shooting and athletic Wildcats by as many as 10 points. But UCLA's defense gave the Bruins a chance to win. They forced three turnovers on Kentucky's final six possessions and scored six straight times down the stretch. With only fifteen seconds left in the game, UCLA trailed by only one point, 81-80, and they had the ball.

The Bruins set up an in-bound play, and Kentucky's defenders quickly converged on Ed O'Bannon. Tyus Edney received the pass, dribbled through traffic, and passed to J. R. Henderson at the last instant. Henderson was fouled with 0.6 left on the clock. Henderson had two shots. Make one, and the game went into overtime. Make two, and the Bruins would win. Miss two, and—well, better not think too much about that.

No one should have worried. Put a ball in his hands to shoot, and Henderson instantly becomes about as hot as Bakersfield in the summertime. He made both free throws, the Bruins won, and Pitino was pretty sure he had just seen something special.

"This game had all the intensity of a championship game," Pitino said.

For the Bruins, the intensity level couldn't have been much higher if it had been shot out of a laser. Ed O'Bannon's preseason conditioning paid off, and he led all scorers with 26 points. His brother Charles had a tough time defending Kentucky's Roderick Rhodes and fouled out with 11:33 to go. That was the bad news. The good news was that the freshman Henderson had a chance to shine. So did UCLA center George Zidek, who began to earn a reputation as an offensive force. Zidek, who had spent a lot of time in the weight room before the season, threw his weight around to finish with 10 rebounds and 16 points, including 7 of UCLA's last 11.

The Bruins didn't have long to enjoy that victory or the next two before they flew into Baton Rouge to the Pete Maravich Assembly Hall to face LSU, another athletic team that seemed to be shooting 3-pointers on the way out of the locker room. But they weren't going to outshoot the Bruins. Ed O'Bannon led the way with 28 points, the Bruins made ten of eighteen 3-pointers, and the defense smothered LSU, causing twenty-six turnovers. UCLA won in a runaway, 92-72.

Next up was George Mason University, which couldn't keep up with Edney. The Bruins won easily, 138-100, with Edney carting off everything that wasn't tied down. UCLA's flashy point guard finished with 11 steals—a school record for thievery.

No question about it, the Bruins already looked like a tournament team on the basis of their nonconference play. But regardless of how good a team looks in the preseason, the real test comes when conference play begins. The Pacific-10 Conference is no exception. It's a fact of Pac-10 basketball life that the one team everybody else likes to beat more than any other is UCLA. There are more rivalries than there were Hatfields and McCoys, especially among the California schools. The Bruins were in for some surprises.

While the Pac-10 Conference was once the object of jokes about low scores and laid-back West Coast basketball games, all of the conference schools now provide more than enough competition to prepare their opponents for the NCAA tournament.

Any doubts about that were erased in the first regular season game the Bruins played against Oregon, an old rival.

UCLA had lost the last game of the 1994 regular season to the Ducks, who had overcome a 13-point Bruin lead in the second half to win 80-79. That was then. This was now.

UCLA played uninspired ball but still led in the second half, 58-46. The Bruins turned the ball over twenty-one times, including seven miscues by the usually reliable Edney.

Oregon fought back and thumped UCLA 82-72. This was no one's idea of the way to begin a drive to the national championship!

The Bruins had some difficulty with the Oregon press, but more than anything, UCLA didn't seem to be mentally prepared to play the conference opener.

Oregon fans treated the game like the Ducks had won the national championship, as hundreds of them stormed the court.

Maybe this loss woke the Bruins up, though, because in the next game, against Oregon State, Harrick started freshman J. R. Henderson against scoring sensation Brent Barry (former NBA scoring champ Rick Barry's son). The stoic Henderson held Barry to eight shots as the Bruins won 87-78.

After beating the two Washington schools at home, UCLA went to Arizona, and an inspired Edney outplayed the Wildcat's star, guard Damon Stoudamire, who was only one for twelve on the 3-point shots that are his trademark.

Next on the Arizona weekend trip for the Bruins was a stop in Tempe to face Arizona State. The Bruins played well and defeated the Sun Devils 85-72. Arizona State was ranked thirteenth in the nation, but George Zidek did a good job defensively against Arizona State's star center Mario Bennett, who was held to 14 points.

The Bruins then went back to Pauley Pavilion and defeated Stanford 77-74. It was the team's third victory over a nationally ranked top-twenty team. More importantly, it boosted the Bruins to number four in the national polls.

UCLA must have felt like Rodney Dangerfield, because they certainly got no respect for their national ranking in their next outing against northern California rivals, the Cal Bears.

UCLA had several scoring runs in the game and led in the second half, 61-58. But Tremain Fowlkes and Jelani Gardner brought the Bears back offensively while their zone defense held the Bruins in check. California pulled away for a 100-93 victory, its third in a row at Pauley Pavilion.

After the loss, UCLA rebounded by beating crosstown rival USC 73-69. The Trojans couldn't handle the O'Bannon brothers in the second half, even though USC had kept the first half close. Cameron Dollar showed his potential when he filled in for his friend Edney, who was suffering from the flu.

The Bruins next defeated Notre Dame. In that game the Fighting Irish took their nickname a little too seriously and committed a hard foul against Tyus Edney. Ed O'Bannon charged to Edney's defense, drawing a technical foul and inspiring his teammates with his display of emotion. They ran up a 92-55 victory against the Irish.

UCLA's next road trip was to the University of Wash-

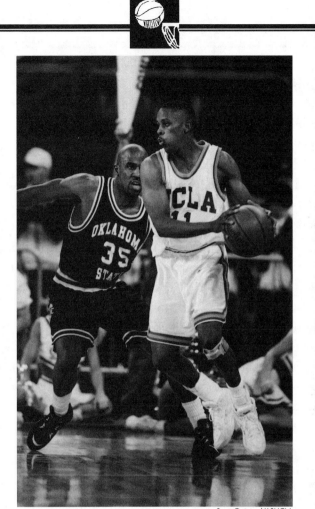

Tyus Edney was the "little bigman" for the 1995 Bruins. One of the fastest players in America his senior year, Tyus "saved the season" for UCLA with his unbelievable full-court drive to score the winning basket against Missouri in the NCAA tournament. Later, he was injured against Oklahoma State and forced to miss most of the championship game against Arkansas.

ington, where they took a side trip to the Kingdome to see where the NCAA Final Four would be played at the end of "March Madness." The Bruins beat the Huskies 74-66, and then headed to Pullman to play Washington State.

That was a great game for Toby Bailey and J.R. Henderson, the two freshmen who combined to score 43 points and sent the Bruins home ecstatic with a 98-83 victory.

Ed O'Bannon then went on a streak that firmly established him as the best player for the best team in the country. In an extremely tough test against Arizona State in Pauley Pavilion, the Bruins won 82-77 in overtime. Ed and his brother Charles took over the game when it went to overtime. Charles made a jump shot, and then Ed got a 3-pointer. Charles went back on defense and blocked a shot, and then George Zidek was fouled and made two free throws.

The "Flying O'Bannon Brothers" were a high-wire act. Ed scored 22 points, and Charles had 23, but deferred to his older brother.

Three days later Ed scored 31 points in thirty-nine minutes against Arizona. The Wildcats tried everything they could to stop him, but he was hotter than Texas chili. The Bruins won a close one, 72-70. The same week, Ed scored 22 points, grabbed 9 rebounds, and blocked five shots against Stanford in an 88-77 Bruin win.

After only two days of rest, UCLA had a rematch with the Bears. Ed O'Bannon tied Reggie Miller's school record by hitting seven 3-point field goals over the Bears's defense. Zidek also had a good game, scoring 22 points. UCLA avenged the earlier loss by thumping the Bears 104-88.

Perhaps the biggest regular-season test of all came at the end of February against perennial power Duke. This game, televised from Pauley Pavilion, helped the Bruins send a message to the rest of America: UCLA was back as a force in college basketball. The Bruins played a zone defense against Duke, which led to turnovers that created a 29-5 scoring run in the second half.

Ed O'Bannon looked like Michael Jordan as he soared to make a two-handed stuff and start the amazing scoring run. Charles O'Bannon and Toby Bailey said later that Ed was back to playing the way he had played in high school before suffering a severe knee injury.

Ed scored 37 points, and the rest of the Bruins showed great balance, with Edney and Charles O'Bannon scoring in double figures—16 and 13 points respectively.

That victory was especially sweet, because Duke had been called "the UCLA of the '90s."

"These games helped the UCLA team believe they could win it all," Assistant Coach Mark Gottfried said afterward.

Following the Duke victory, the Bruins beat Louisville and former UCLA Assistant Coach Denny Crum, 91-73. Freshman Toby Bailey and sophomore Charles O'Bannon led the scoring for the Bruins. Even though Louisville's defense tried to take away the fast break, UCLA responded every time Louisville got close. UCLA also proved that its half-court set offense was just as powerful as their fast break.

The Bruins won two more games during the regular season, finishing with thirteen consecutive victories and a record of 25-2. UCLA was chosen as the number one seed in the NCAA west regional. The stage was now set for another championship quest.

March Madness

7

The NCAA men's basketball tournament is often called March Madness—a wild series of single elimination, heart-stopping, nail-biting games between college basketball's best teams.

Each year there's a Cinderella story or two, as well as controversy over several of the sixty-four picks. Usually the major powers in the sport make the field. Millions of basketball fans watch this spectacle, and eventually a champion emerges on a nationally televised prime-time Monday-night game.

In 1995, UCLA was the top seed in the West, having won the Pac-10 Conference. In fact, the team finished the season also ranked number one in the country. The Bruins had finished the regular season with a thirteen-game winning streak.

The team's first-round opponent

was a college many had never heard of—Florida International University (FIU). UCLA might have been tempted to take the Golden Panthers of FIU—with their 11-18 record—lightly if it were not for the painful memory of the previous year's opening game 112-102 loss to Tulsa, a low point for the Bruins. This time the players had a healthy enough fear to be alert.

No first-round accident would befall UCLA this time. The Bruins took control early over an outmanned FIU team, led 43-23 at the half, and cruised to a 92-56 victory. Henderson led the way with 16 points. Tyus Edney had 8 points and 8 assists. The Bruins outshot the Golden Panthers 60 percent to 34 percent and outrebounded FIU 47-26.

Toby Bailey told the media afterwards that he thought the first game against FIU was particularly difficult because "we didn't want to be caught off guard."

The UCLA bench enjoyed this game, because every reserve played at least five minutes and scored at least 2 points. Many basketball fans expected that UCLA would be playing Indiana in the second-round game, but the University of Missouri Tigers surprised a lot of folks by eliminating the Hoosiers.

Missouri's 6′2″ guard, Paul O'Liney, an excellent outside shooter, scored 22 points, and Indiana had all sorts of problems with the Tigers's two seven-foot brothers, Sammie and Simeon Haley. Indiana went down 65-60, provoking some postgame hysterics from Coach Bobby Knight.

After having such an easy test in the first game, UCLA could have taken Missouri for granted and paid the price. Missouri was something else in the first half, especially from 3-point range, where they were seven of eleven for 64 percent! O'Liney was outstanding for the Tigers, making all four of the 3-pointers he attempted and missing only one shot. He went six for seven from the field and ended up with 16 points.

At the half, UCLA was a bit dazed and trailed 42-34. But the players seemed to wake up in the second half, and with slightly more than two minutes to go in the game, they trailed 72-69. Ed O'Bannon hit a jumper that cut the lead to 1 point. O'Liney tried to counter with a 3-point shot, but he missed. O'Bannon rebounded and was fouled. He sank both free throws to give the Bruins a 73-72 lead with less than a minute left.

Missouri Coach Norm Stewart decided to hold the ball for the last shot and go for the win. Kendrick Moore of Missouri ran the clock down and got the ball inside to Julian Winfield for a surprisingly easy bucket. The Missouri bench and fans went wild. Now, with only 4.8 seconds remaining, it looked like UCLA's season was about to end in misery again.

What the Tigers didn't know was that UCLA practices for just this situation. The Bruins drill on dribbling the length of the floor and getting off a shot in under six seconds. Tyus Edney knew he could do it in less than the 4.8 seconds left on the game clock.

But practice is one thing, and an NCAA tournament game—with thousands of screaming fans—is another. In the huddle during the time-out, Tyus heard Ed O'Bannon say, "We're going to win!"

Cameron Dollar passed the ball in to Edney, his friend, mentor, and teammate, and for Tyus it was "center stage." He took the ball quickly past midcourt, and in a move that would have done Pete Maravich proud, whipped the ball behind his back on the dribble and momentarily froze Missouri's defenders.

Then Edney went into the lane against Missouri's 6'9", 215-pound Derek Grimm, who had his arms up so as not to foul. Like Jack climbing the Beanstalk, Edney leaped mightily, and at the top of his jump—with his right hand outstretched—he flicked the ball around Grimm and off the glass. *Nothing but net!* The buzzer sounded. UCLA won 75-74.

Dollar, Henderson, and Bailey, who were trailing on the play, started jumping up and down. Grimm and the other Missouri players were stunned. Ed O'Bannon lifted his arms in exultation. "It was just a great feeling to know that the ball went in, and we were still in the tournament," Edney said later.

Coach Wooden says every team that wins the NCAA needs to be a little lucky. Maybe the Bruins were fortunate to win with 4.8 seconds on the clock, but Edney's play was "all-pro."

After their reprieve, the Bruins were determined not

Scott Quintard/ASUCLA

The younger of the high-flying O'Bannon brothers, Charles surrendered much of the limelight to brother Ed during the 1995 season. Here he puts up a one-hander against Arkansas in the title game. With Ed departed to the pros, Charles no longer has to play the "little brother" role for the Bruins. Look out!

to take anyone else lightly. Some sports commentators thought that the Bruins's next opponent, Mississippi State, would dominate UCLA inside with their outstanding 6'11", 255-pound sophomore center, Erick Dampier. Instead, George Zidek and Ed O'Bannon sandwiched Dampier defensively and allowed him only 11 points. Ed O'Bannon led the Bruins with 21 points in twenty-nine minutes.

Edney had another great game with his patented spin moves and drives inside against Dampier, the shot blocker. Edney was too quick for him and forced Dampier to pick up two fouls in the first four minutes.

Cameron Dollar later said Edney shot him a look the first time he drove on Dampier that said, "We're ready to roll, baby. Let's do it again." And so they did.

The Bruins ran up a 21-point halftime lead against Mississippi State, 40-19, and won going away, 86-67.

UCLA's semifinal matchup would be against Connecticut. In 1995 the Huskies had great men's and women's basketball teams. The big story before the tournament was that U Conn might be the first school ever to win both men's and women's NCAA titles in one sport in the same year.

There has long been a debate between the East and West Coast as to which part of the country has better college basketball. It goes back to the fifties. Former UCLA Assistant Coach Jerry Norman tells the history of this East versus West basketball argument.

Jerry Norman:

"All the New York schools in the '50s were the top teams in the country, because all the good New York players stayed in New York. They didn't go to places like North Carolina or Duke. They went to St. Johns, NYU, CCNY, and Long Island."

According to Norman, though, the California schools were just as good and held their own whenever they met any of those East Coast powers. But there was no ESPN, and all the major media were based in New York City. UCLA, Cal State, Stanford, and USC didn't get their deserved recognition.

The balance of power in college basketball changed when UCLA won its first titles in 1964 and 1965, because these victories were a key factor in turning Kareem Abdul-Jabbar away from the New York schools. After UCLA continued to win, there weren't too many top players in the country they didn't have a shot at recruiting.

The East-versus-West battle continues to this day. Just before the Connecticut-UCLA game, U Conn Coach Jim Calhoun said Edney wasn't as fast as Georgetown guard Allen Iverson. (Connecticut had played Georgetown in the Big East and defeated them.) Someone put Calhoun's statement up on a bulletin board in the UCLA locker room.

That may have given Edney some extra incentive to

show Coach Calhoun what he could do. Or maybe Edney just wanted to let people know that he and UCLA weren't going to be stopped in the regionals after their miraculous win against Missouri.

At the pregame press conference, Connecticut star Donny Marshall repeated Coach Calhoun's comments that East Coast basketball is tougher than West Coast basketball. UCLA proved them wrong.

Tyus led the team in a fantastic game against the Huskies. Connecticut tried to pressure him, but in the open court he is next to impossible to contain.

The Bruins trailed by 6 points early in the first half, but came back to take the lead and hold it for the remainder of the half. But not without some excitement. U Conn's splendid Ray Allen hit a 3-pointer to cut the UCLA lead to 45-41 with only 3.6 seconds to go in the first half. Just then, Charles O'Bannon called a time-out. Harrick was furious because he considered the time-out wasted.

Who would the Bruins go to in this situation? Why, Calhoun's favorite Bruin, of course. Dollar in-bounded the ball to Edney, who dribbled downcourt like a runaway pinball, screeched to a halt twenty-five feet from the hoop, and drilled a 3-pointer. The Bruins finished the half up by 7.

Calhoun was speechless. Harrick wasn't. Remember that wasted time-out? Not anymore. Like the coach who yells "No!" when he sees a player pull up to shoot a thirty-footer, then immediately says "Great shot!" when it

Scott Quintard/ASUCLA

Cameron Dollar, point guard, was a capable backup to Tyus
Edney during the 1995 season. When Tyus could not play in the
championship game against Arkansas because of a badly
sprained wrist, Cameron had to take his place in a pressure-
packed situation. The first time he handled the ball, it was stolen
by an Arkansas player who scored an easy layup. Cameron
fought through the jitters and helped lead UCLA to victory.

goes in, Harrick changed his mind about that "wasted" time-out.

"Head's up time-out call," Harrick told Charles. After all, it's a coach's prerogative to change his mind—especially when you're winning!

In the second half, Edney and Bailey led the offensive charge. Edney finished with 22 points and 10 assists. Bailey and his high-wire act led the scoring with 26 points. On defense, Ed O'Bannon held U Conn star Donny Marshall to 15 points. J. R. Henderson, Bailey's fellow freshman, also had an outstanding game with 18 points. The final score was 102-96. Tyus Edney was named the MVP for the west regional.

At last, the Bruins were headed back to the Final Four. Ed O'Bannon celebrated by cutting down the net from the UCLA basket while a couple hundred Bruin fans cheered him on.

It was clear, though, that the Bruins and their fans were already dreaming of another net awaiting them in the great Northwest. They hoped there would be more than the law of gravity bringing it down.

The Final Four

8

At the end of March 1995, a tournament that started with sixty-four teams in men's college basketball had wound down to just four—perhaps the most elite group in all of college sports—"The Final Four."

Any team that makes it to this select group is good. The 1995 teams were no exception, each having an abundance of great players who arrived in Seattle ready to battle in the Kingdome for bragging rights as "the national champions." Here's a brief look at the final four and their road to Seattle.

NORTH CAROLINA

Seeded number two in the southeast regional, the Tarheels are a perennial contender, making their third appearance in the Final Four in the last five years. Their coach is the legendary Dean Smith, who is such an institution in Chapel Hill, the basketball arena is known as the "Dean Dome." Smith preaches team play. In his thirty-four years as the head man at North Carolina, Smith has coached some of basketball's finest players, including Michael Jordan and James Worthy. Jordan is probably the greatest one-on-one player in basketball, but when he played for the Tarheels, he was a team player like everyone in Coach Smith's system.

Dean Smith's team in 1995 was led by outstanding sophomores Jerry Stackhouse and Rasheed Wallace.

The Tarheels had been ranked number one in the polls six weeks during the regular season, but to get to the Final Four, they had to beat their old rival, Kentucky. The North Carolina-Kentucky matchup paired the two schools with the most victories in the history of college basketball. The number-one seeded Kentucky jumped out to an early 8-2 lead but trailed at the half 34-31. North Carolina stayed ahead the rest of the way and went home with the southeast title to prepare for another trip to the finals in Seattle.

ARKANSAS

The defending national champion, with all its starters back, was an experienced and confident group. The prior season's Final Four MVP, Corliss "the Big Nasty" Williamson, at 6'7" and 245 pounds, led the Razorbacks into the tournament averaging 20 points and 7.5 rebounds per game. Corliss was a collegiate version of the Phoenix Suns's Charles Barkley; both can score and are great rebounders and team leaders.

Guard Corey Beck was the heart and soul of the team, while Scotty Thurman is one of the premier 3-point shooters in the country.

It isn't surprising how confident the Razorbacks were about repeating as champions. Arkansas had a strong bench and a "forty minutes of hell" full-court press that usually wore their opponents down and out.

Yet with both these factors going for them, the Razorbacks had still needed to have more breaks than any team in the tournament to make it to the Final Four. Arkansas's journey to the Final Four wasn't easy.

In the first round, the Razorbacks almost lost to Texas Southern but pulled the game out 79-78. The second-round game with Syracuse was almost as close. Syracuse would have won had it not been for a mental mistake by one of the Orangemen who, with possession of the ball, could have let the clock run out but instead called a time-out. That allowed the Razorbacks to tie and send the game into overtime. Arkansas squeaked it out, 96-94.

After dodging bullets in the early rounds, the Razorbacks beat Memphis State in overtime and then cruised to a 7-point win over Virginia in the finals of the midwest regionals. At last the Razorbacks were on their way to Seattle and a chance to repeat as national champs.

OKLAHOMA STATE

The Cowboys—led by 6'11", 292-pound senior Bryant "Big Country" Reeves and long-range bomber Randy Rutherford—became the fourth seed in the east regional. They had a twenty-win season for the fifth straight year, and veteran coach Eddie Sutton was optimistic of his team's chances to go all the way.

Reeves was a great shooter for a big man, said to have soft hands and a gentle touch on his shots, particularly those close to the basket. His appetite for rebounding was prodigious.

Oklahoma State had a tremendous defense, having held their opponents under 40 percent shooting from the field in ten of their last twelve games. They upset top-seeded Wake Forest in the semifinals 71-66. In their regional finals they beat a formidable University of Massachusetts team after trailing at the half. In the second half they held U Mass to 26.7 percent shooting and won by 14 points, 68-54. The Cowboys were on their way to the Final Four for the first time since 1951.

UCLA

The Bruins were the only top-seeded team in a regional to make it to the Final Four. They were also the top-ranked team in the country.

UCLA ran past Florida International 92-56 to set up the heart-stopper against Missouri. Tyus Edney was the

Scott Quintard/ASUCLA

As the championship game wound down, every UCLA basket received this kind of explosive reaction from the Bruin bench.

man as he beat the clock on a mad dash with 4.8 seconds to play and the Bruins down by a point. He banked home the game winner.

Next up was Mississippi State. Behind Ed O'Bannon's team-leading 21 points and 8 rebounds, the Bruins cruised to a 19-point victory.

In the western regional final game, freshman Toby Bailey exploded for 26 points to lead the Bruins to the regional crown over an excellent University of Connecticut team.

On Friday, March 31, 1995, the day before the Final Four semifinals, all the teams worked out in the Kingdome. Everyone in Seattle was soon talking about how Bryant "Big Country" Reeves had announced his presence with authority by shattering a backboard—"Shaq style"—during layups. Reeves's teammates scattered to protect themselves from the flying glass. It was the first time in the history of the Final Four that a backboard had been broken.

After hearing of Reeves's feat, George Zidek, UCLA's 250-pound center, who mimics Arnold Schwarzennegger's "The Terminator," said it was also *his* dream to break a backboard! It was not to be. (Not yet, anyway.) But during their workout on the Kingdome floor, the Bruins displayed the conditioning, quickness, and team precision that had gotten them back to the top of the mountain for the first time in fifteen years.

Although focused in their practice, the Bruins were anything but boring. Toby Bailey had his share of turnaround slam dunks, Ed and Charles O'Bannon threw a few down, and Zidek dropped one hook shot after another softly through the nets. What stood out the most, though, was the camaraderie of the Bruin team.

The UCLA-Oklahoma State semifinal game was billed as "Big Country against Foreign Country," referring to 292-pound Reeves and 250-pound Zidek, a native of the former Czechoslovakia. A number of the coaches reminisced that the game recalled the playing style of teams led by legendary coaches John Wooden and Henry Iba (former Oklahoma State and U.S. Olympic coach).

Tyus got the Bruins off to a quick start with their first 3 points and 5 of the first 7. UCLA's biggest lead was 9—with 13:34 left in the half, the score was 20-11. But "Big Country" was too much for anybody to handle as he single-handedly kept the Cowboys in the game with 18 first-half points—the only player in double figures for Oklahoma State.

But even with Reeves's domination, the half belonged to Tyus, the Bruins's "Little General." He had 10 points and 5 assists. And he also had the shot of the game.

Late in the first half, after Tyus received a pass from Cameron Dollar on a UCLA fast break, he flew to the basket, and with a defender blocking his path, spun in midair and flipped the ball back over his head with a touch of English. The ball kissed the glass and fell through, to the delight of his high-fiving and backslapping teammates on the bench. The half ended in a tie, 37-37.

During his halftime talk, Coach Harrick was upbeat. "You didn't think this was going to be easy did you?" he asked. Then he urged his troops to concentrate on the boards, the place where Oklahoma State had staked its claim to a 19-8 rebounding edge.

The Cowboys briefly took the lead early in the second half, but then the Bruins's defense took over. UCLA was down by 3 when the pressure started to pay off with an 11-0 run. The Cowboys retaliated with a 9-0 flurry of their own to take the lead back by a point with 9:33 to go.

Both teams played tough, and then Edney took over again. The little bigman scored 11 of his team-high 21 points in the final eight minutes, and the Bruins ran the game out with 12 unanswered points. Add it all up, and it was a 74-61 UCLA victory.

Zidek, Henderson, and the O'Bannon brothers did an outstanding job of controlling Reeves in the second half, holding him to only 7 points.

As great a victory as it was, the Bruins didn't get much of a chance to enjoy it before they got the bad news. Tyus Edney was hurt. UCLA's floor general had badly sprained his right wrist and was almost certainly going to miss the championship game. This was not how it was supposed to

Ed O'Bannon, the emotional leader of the 1995 Bruins, gives his kid brother Charles a hug after UCLA won the title game. After Charles, one of the most highly sought players in the nation as a high school senior, selected UCLA, Ed told him: "Let's go win a national championship."

be. How could the Bruins play for the NCAA title without Tyus? It would be like trying to start your car without a battery.

Somehow, though, the Bruins would just have to get it done. After all, it's not very often you have a chance to win a national championship. In UCLA's case, it had been twenty years. If Edney was to be out, then so be it, said the Bruins, who agreed that it was about time to change a little history.

In the other Final Four semifinal game between Arkansas and North Carolina, the Tarheels appeared to be in trouble early when their star forward, Jerry Stackhouse, injured his thigh on the first possession of the game. But they hung in behind Jeff McInnis's 21 first-half points and took the lead at the half, 46-39. Arkansas was frigid in the first half, shooting just 30 percent. Corliss Williamson, their MVP, had the most trouble, with only 2 points— shooting one of five from the floor.

The Razorbacks warmed up in the second half, though, with Williamson leading the way. During one eight-minute stretch, Corliss accounted for 13 points to boost Arkansas's lead to 60-52 with nine minutes to go in the game.

The Tarheels came back to within 1 point, 69-68, with forty-eight seconds to play before Arkansas closed with a

6-0 run. Corliss Williamson scored 19 points in the second half to help send Dean Smith and UNC back to Chapel Hill.

For the fifth straight game, Nolan Richardson's Razorbacks had come from behind to pull out a victory.

The stage was now set. The Final Four was now the Final Two. In one corner, the team who was the defending champion. In the other corner, the one with the richest basketball tradition in the country. Something had to give. No one had to wait very long to find out.

Cut Down the Nets

9

Before the Arkansas Razorbacks took the court to defend their NCAA basketball title, the team huddled together and yelled "Showtime!"

In the other dressing room, the UCLA Bruins huddled together and talked about playing together as a team.

The difference in emphasis may explain why UCLA eventually cut down the nets and celebrated the victory while Arkansas left the court in silence.

John Wooden had always stressed teamwork. That was one of the reasons there were ten championship banners hanging in Pauley Pavilion. The 1995 Bruins believed just as much in "the team" as any of Wooden's clubs, but as Charles O'Bannon pointed out after the title game, "We didn't have a Walton or an Alcindor, and we didn't have an

Edney. But we had a team full of guys with big hearts."

Although twenty years had passed since Coach Wooden had brought a Bruin team to the title game, his influence remained.

Wooden had advised UCLA Coach Jim Harrick, and Harrick later shared that advice with the media. Perhaps the most important insight Wooden had given concerned criticism and praise.

"I love John Wooden," said Harrick. "He's the wisest man I've ever known, and he has taught me so much, hundreds of things. But the most important thing he told me is that if I listen to too much criticism, it will hurt my coaching, and if I listen to too much praise, it will hurt my coaching."

Wooden was offered the opportunity to speak to the 1995 team before they went into battle against Arkansas, but he declined, deliberately choosing to stay in the background. "They had a tremendous season," he told the media, "and I didn't want to take any attention away from them." Instead, Coach Wooden, eighty-four years young, took a seat in the Kingdome crowd, the guest of one of the wealthiest men in America—Microsoft's founder, Bill Gates.

Harrick shares Wooden's philosophy of emphasizing team, as do Harrick's assistant coaches. And the players who are leaders on the floor, like Ed O'Bannon, have gotten the message.

Earlier in the season, after a personally frustrating

game, freshman Toby Bailey had played only ten minutes and scored a single point. He was sitting quietly by himself with his head lowered. Ed O'Bannon spotted him and wondered why he wasn't celebrating with his teammates after a close win. "It's about team!" he reminded Toby.

For Assistant Coach Lorenzo Romar, Ed's response clearly reflected the kind of leader O'Bannon was for UCLA in 1995. It also fit in with the concept of "team as family" that Romar helped bring to UCLA when he signed on as an assistant in 1992. "Ed was such a leader for this team that there were times he took us on his back and carried us and wouldn't let us lose," Romar said.

Ed O'Bannon's leadership knew no boundaries. Locker room, practices, games, everywhere Ed was, he showed the way. Just before the Bruins were going to run onto the Kingdome court to play the championship game, they stood in a darkened tunnel, waiting for their cue. Ed chose this time to address them. He didn't offer any pep talk or any deep advice. He just said one sentence: "Fellas, it's just a pickup game."

Of course, it wasn't, but O'Bannon had at once cut through the tension, put everyone at ease, and said, without actually saying it, that everything would be just fine if everyone played his normal game.

This is what a leader does. And make no mistake, Ed O'Bannon is a leader.

Coaches like John Wooden and Jim Harrick emphasize fundamentals, make sure players are in good condition, and stress team play. Some basketball commentators actually criticized UCLA players during the season for passing the ball too much and being *too* unselfish! They felt that Edney should be penetrating more, and that the O'Bannons and Bailey should have more of a chance to show off their individual skills.

"When people criticize us for being unselfish, I think that is a compliment to the team," said Assistant Coach Romar. According to him, young basketball players' heads are often filled with messages they get from basketball-related television advertising—messages that tend to glorify individual accomplishments at the expense of the team. They are told to "Be like Mike," the superstar Michael Jordan, or "I am not a role model" Charles Barkley.

"We are a close-knit family," Charles O'Bannon told the media in talking about the Bruins. "We feel it is us against the world, and that no one thinks we can achieve what we believe we can achieve. We use that as a motivation to help us achieve our goals."

The Bruins had plenty of motivation and many opportunities on championship night to display the team/family concept, as opposed to the "showtime" concept, of playing basketball.

Scott Quintard/ASUCLA

Coach Jim Harrick and the Bruins accept the NCAA title trophy at the Kingdome in Seattle, minutes after defeating the defending champion Arkansas Razorbacks, 89-78. Like all coaches at UCLA since the end of the John Wooden era, Harrick has endured a full dose of criticism. How sweet it is!

Their first opportunity came early in the Arkansas game when Tyus Edney tried gamely to play with his severely sprained right wrist. Tyus started, but he left the game after two minutes and thirty-seven seconds, never to return. Cameron Dollar, Edney's confident replacement, came in and promptly had the ball stolen for a layup.

CBS-TV commentator Billy Packer said after the steal, "We talked about ninety-four feet of hell, and without Edney in the game, that hell is really going to come now."

Cameron was trying not to be nervous. He remembered Ed O'Bannon's words before the game.

Arkansas led 16-10 as Dollar was getting his nerves settled. Ed O'Bannon brought the Bruins back into the game and then into the lead with a dunk on a fast break—the first of many to come.

Williamson, 1994's Final Four MVP, had a rough night. He tried to outmuscle Zidek, the Bruins's big center, but never got his game together. He ended up shooting just three for sixteen for 12 points with only 4 rebounds.

UCLA was up 40-39 at halftime and was able to hold the lead throughout the second half. Williamson brought the Razorbacks to within 3 points with 5:22 to go, 67-64. Then the Bruins put on a 10-1 spurt. They never looked back and finished it up 89-78.

Ed O'Bannon, named Final Four MVP, did everything the Bruins could have asked from their leader: He ran, dunked, played defense, rebounded, and encouraged his teammates all night long, finishing with a game-high 30 points and 17 rebounds. Toby Bailey put on a high-flying act that probably needed a flight plan. Toby and the Bruin fast breaks were so spectacular that most of the 38,540 Kingdome fans will probably never forget them. The energetic, kinetic Bailey had a season-tying 26 points and snatched 9 rebounds.

Coach Harrick used only six players (excluding Edney) and showed the country that the finely conditioned, disciplined, and exciting Bruins were back.

All seven of the Bruins were spectacular:

- Edney was the head cheerleader of the group, the encourager for Cameron Dollar, the wounded general pulling for his troops.
- Dollar came through in the clutch. After two years of going head-to-head with the quickest and fastest guard in the country every day in practice, when his time came he played like a veteran. He had 6 points, 8 assists, and only 3 turnovers in the pressure game of the season.
- Henderson, in seventeen minutes had 2 points, 2 rebounds, and a blocked shot.
- Bailey tied his season high in points with 26 and spent most of the game doing what he does best— running the break and bringing the crowd to its feet with spectacular, gymnastic slam dunks.
- Zidek had the game of his life against Williamson,

last year's MVP, holding him scoreless for a thirty-three-minute stretch and a three of sixteen shooting performance. Zidek had wanted to go home to the Czech Republic after a disappointing sophomore season. Was he glad he had stayed!

- Charles O'Bannon did what a little brother is supposed to do—let his big brother be the star but help wherever needed. And help he did! From his first block on Williamson to his 11 points, 9 rebounds, 6 assists, and 2 steals.

- Ed O'Bannon was indeed the star. He had been waiting since he tore up his knee five years earlier to show the world what he could do. He saved the best for last: forty minutes, 30 points, 17 rebounds, 3 assists, and 3 steals. It was about as complete a game as anyone could play.

Coach Harrick said afterwards that Ed O'Bannon was the best college basketball player in America. There weren't many who would disagree after a performance like that one.

Harrick's stars left the collective mark they wanted to as a team. When it was all over, play-by-play announcer Jim Nantz told the nationwide television audience, "This is what team play is all about."

After the scoreboard horn sounded, a brass band began to play wildly, as if the circus had come to town. The UCLA Bruins were champions again!

Pandemonium erupted. Soon the floor was crowded with ecstatic players and cheerleaders.

Amid this sea of excitement and celebration, a peaceful circle formed. At its center was UCLA Assistant Coach Lorenzo Romar, on his knees, leading the players in a prayer of gratitude. Coach Romar was not alone at center court. Most of the UCLA players were with him, on their knees, holding hands and smiling as the prayer became a giant group hug. Tears of joy mingled with sweat from the toil of a hard-won victory.

Ed O'Bannon was asked by CBS's Nantz what it was like to play without Edney.

"We stayed positive the whole time," O'Bannon replied. "We put everything in God's hands. We walk by faith and not by sight; that's how it is."

When Ed's father was interviewed on a Los Angeles postgame show, he said, "We're going to cherish this moment." While O'Bannon Sr. was being interviewed, the UCLA marching band chanted in the background, "Have more kids! Have more kids!"

Ed O'Bannon deflected the spotlight from himself after winning the Most Outstanding Player award for the tournament and called teammate Tyus Edney to the platform to share the honor.

Ed said, "Tyus was behind us. He brought us here. The MVP goes to Tyus Edney. Tyus is the man."

It was unquestionably tough for Tyus to watch the championship game without being able to play and give his best effort. After the game, Harrick said, "Up until tonight, Tyus had the best tournament performance of any player. Even from the bench, he was helping encourage all of us."

Zidek praised the team in his Czeck-accented English and was so happy he even danced on the podium when he took his place for the trophy presentation.

After the interviews, sportscaster Nantz told the Bruins, "There are some nets waiting for you. Go cut them down."

At the trophy ceremony, Jim Harrick paid tribute to the fans who had made their way to Seattle's Kingdome. Later, in an open letter to UCLA fans, he wrote, "Winning in basketball is like winning in life. You dream. You work hard to achieve those dreams. You find courage to overcome the obstacles to those dreams. And you discover peace in your heart when you reach the pinnacle of those dreams and realize your best is good enough."

Harrick also passed out praise to the UCLA players, the ones busy cutting down the nets.

"This is the finest bunch of student-athletes I have ever been associated with. They're students, they are great, great people, and they are fine athletes," Harrick wrote.

Before leaving Westwood to travel to the Final Four in Seattle, Coach Harrick had asked the team to stand at center court at Pauley Pavilion and look at the ten championship banners that hang from the arena's rafters. He had told the team they had an opportunity to bring another championship banner home. The players had gazed quietly at the banners, realizing that they could be part of history.

Now the long wait was over. The 1995 Bruins would travel back to Westwood and add another banner to the ceiling of Pauley Pavilion.

The O'Bannon family enjoys a cherished moment with the 1995 trophy. Charles, Ed Sr. (a wide receiver on the 1971 UCLA football team), mother Madeline, and 1995 NCAA finals MVP Ed Jr. are all smiles. And shouldn't they be?!

Reflections— on Why UCLA Won Again

10

Without question, many factors contributed to the return of the basketball championship to UCLA: talented, motivated players working as a team; superb coaches who wisely prepared their players; hard work by everybody; enthusiastic fans, friends, and family members; and, of course, good fortune—you always need some of that.

But there is another factor in UCLA's success in 1995 that deserves some attention. A number of the Bruin players and coaches participated in Bible study, prayer, and other activities that bonded these men together spiritually. After winning the championship game, a number of them gave public thanks to God for their success.

I understood clearly why they would do this, although that was not always the case with me. When I played at UCLA and later in the NBA, I was not that interested in spiritual matters.

I've always been a person who asks questions, though not necessarily out loud. I guess I could be described as a seeker, someone who must know the "why" about life.

When I was still quite young, healthy, strong, and fun loving, with my future (it seemed like forever) ahead of me, my grandmother died. That event intensified my questions. She was gone, and she didn't come back. Where did she go? Would I ever see her again? I had no answers.

The years went by, and things went well for me. As I look back, it seems as though someone was directing the events of my life.

I ended up at UCLA because it was the only four-year school that offered me a scholarship. I didn't know anything about the school, its athletic history, or its basketball coach. Of course, Coach Wooden ended up being, perhaps, the finest basketball coach ever. I played on UCLA's first two NCAA championship teams. I also played on the Olympic volleyball team in Tokyo at the age of twenty, then in the NBA for twelve years—five of them in my hometown, Los Angeles, with the Lakers.

It seemed life could not get any better! I played with and against some of the greatest athletes in history: Elgin Baylor, Jerry West, Wilt Chamberlain, Bill Russell, Oscar Robertson, and others. I was married to a beautiful woman who really loved me. She and I traveled around the world, had money, investments, and fame.

Still in my twenties, I was on top of the world. There was nothing else the world had to offer that could have added to my happiness and fulfillment.

But whenever I slowed down long enough to think about life, I still had questions that weren't being answered. Why was I here? Where was I going? These questions were heavy on my mind.

I seriously started looking for the answers to those questions my second year in the NBA. My search took me from a Ouija board to tarot cards, astrology, cults, the occult, and finally to witchcraft. I had a large library on these topics and more.

But in every area I looked, something seemed wrong or didn't make sense. I kept searching.

After a basketball camp in 1972, I started meeting with a man who had spoken at the camp. He was an expert on nutrition and conditioning. We met daily to work out, eat a healthy lunch, and talk. I had questions, and he had answers. Eventually, my questions turned from health and conditioning to the spiritual.

One day, to answer one of my questions, he pulled a Bible from his desk drawer, opened it to a specific page, and gave me a logical answer to my question. This pattern continued for days.

Using his Bible as the source book, my friend told me about God and how great and awesome He is—that He created the universe and everything in it, including me. I learned that He controls the times and the seasons, the stars and the seas.

What an adventure my quest had become! I was referred to a local church where the pastor taught the Bible with clarity. As I heard more, I had more questions. The same ones people are asking today. "What's going wrong in our society?" "Why are things getting worse?" "Why can't people get along?"

Look at our world. The Serbs and the Croats, the Arabs and the Jews, the Blacks and the Whites—all at war. There is anger, strife, hatred, abuse, killings, and prejudice everywhere. Why was Rodney King beaten the way he was? Why would Mark Fuhrman say the things he said that disrupted the O. J. Simpson trial? Why would a group of young punks open fire on a car that made a wrong turn in L.A. and kill a three-year-old child? Why gangs? Why drugs? Why murder?

There is an answer! It's an old answer that some people think is dated—but it's not. It's called sin—sin within each of us. What else could cause us to hate one another, to kill one another?

Here are some things the Bible has to say about it:

There is none righteous, no, not one. . . .

There is none who does good, no, not one. . . .
All have sinned and fall short of the glory of God. . . .
The wages of sin is death. *

These words apply to all of us.

But God has provided a remedy for the problem of sin—Jesus Christ, His Son, who condescended to become a man. He lived a perfect life without sin, which fulfilled God's requirement. Then He went to a cross, taking the sin of the world upon Himself and completing His sacrifice for us.

God has explained all of this in His Word, the Bible. It's the greatest story ever told! And it has changed my life completely.

When I was twenty-nine, I for the first time really understood that I was a sinner in need of help—a Savior. And Jesus Christ was that Savior. He died for me.

When God helped me understand all of this, I asked Jesus Christ to be my Savior and Lord, and through His generosity and kindness, I became a new person. I now have answers to my questions.

If we are in right relationship with God through Jesus Christ, when we die we will spend eternity with Him in heaven. We don't have to fear death anymore.

And as to why I'm here, it's to give glory to Him. I still fall short, and will until the day I die, but I now have a

*Rom. 3:10, 12, 23; 6:23

deep peace and indescribable joy and a desire to do what's right in God's eyes.

Because Jesus Christ means everything to me, I was thrilled to hear that faith was important to many of those connected with the UCLA team.

One of them was Assistant Coach Lorenzo Romar, a devout Christian. A soft-spoken, humble man who once played in the NBA, Coach Romar knows that it takes more than conditioning and talent—not only to win, but to prepare players for life off the basketball court.

Coach Romar sees himself as a mentor to young men. His purpose is to build team unity. He invests his time in the players' lives, so they will be better players on the court and better men off the court.

Like so many young people today, some of UCLA's players don't have a father or mother or are far away from their homes and parents. Lorenzo takes a special interest in these players and spends extra time with them.

According to Coach Harrick, Romar has the ability to communicate well with players and their parents. "He's really good at talking to recruits," Harrick has told the Los Angeles media.

At practice, Coach Romar handles the guards and the

Scott Quintard/ASUCLA

Coach Jim Harrick gets a post-game shower. Do you think he'll mind having to send the suit to the cleaners?

3-point shooting situations. "His one-on-one and group teaching skills are top-notch," said Harrick.

When he was growing up, Lorenzo's parents encouraged his involvement in basketball. The shooting skills he developed led to a scholarship offer from the University of Washington, where NBA scout Pete Newell saw him and encouraged the Golden State Warriors to draft him.

Lorenzo's own playing philosophy changed during his four years as a guard with Golden State and the Milwaukee Bucks.

"Before I became a Christian, I thought I was really something," he said. "I specialized in trash-talking and being a showboat player. If the other teams and coaches didn't notice me, I made sure they did by telling them how great I was."

Romar's life changed after attending a Bible study for players and their wives when he was with the Warriors. "My wife and I came from religious backgrounds, but we never read the Bible and we never knew we had so much to learn about God," said Lorenzo. "It brought us closer together, and we became thrilled with God. We dedicated our lives to Christ and to Christian service at that Bible study."

After playing two years for Milwaukee, Romar received an invitation to play and work for Athletes in Action (AIA)—a highly competitive Christian basketball team. He played for AIA for three years before taking on the role of player/coach for the team. As a player and coach, he spent another four years with AIA.

Coach Romar is an excellent recruiter, and his faith—as well as that of former Assistant Coach Mark Gottfried—has been a key factor in UCLA's ability to draw recruits. Cameron Dollar says that the Christian faith of Gottfried (also once an AIA player) and Romar influenced him to choose UCLA.

"Their spiritual background was a key reason for my coming here," said Dollar.

Through his basketball ability, Cameron gained admittance to a private high school in Maryland in his junior year. "My assistant coach there, Kevin Sutton, took me to a wonderful interdenominational church where I committed my life to Christ," he said. "Through AIA summer camps I have been taught to play for an audience of one: Jesus Christ."

Cameron rejects the stereotype of Christian athletes as unaggressive on the field or on the court.

"I challenge anyone to look at tapes of my games since I became a Christian and say that I'm not a more aggressive player!" Dollar said. "I want to give my all for Jesus Christ every time I'm out on the court, even though I have more ambitions now than just being a basketball player."

Tyus Edney (who was drafted by the NBA's Sacramento Kings) and Cameron have decided to meet together to grow further in their Christian life.

Other Bruin players appreciate the influence of

Lorenzo Romar. "Lorenzo has been a great friend as well as a father figure, even though I have a dad," said star forward Charles O'Bannon. "When he recruited me, he told me he was going to help me mature as a man, and he has. He's been in the NBA, and he knows what it takes to get there as far as a work ethic is concerned."

J. R. Henderson said, "Coach Romar helped hold this team together through the season as a family by being committed to God and basketball and showing how that relates to the Bible."

If Romar is successful, it really isn't all due to what he says. "Over half of what these players learn from me isn't the result of anything I say, but what they see in my life," he said.

Another key person who contributed to the spiritual strength of the Bruins was Mike Bunkley, the chaplain to the team. Bunkley conducted the Bible study and chapel programs that as many as ten UCLA players attended each week.

Before the national championship game, a special chapel service was held, and many of the players attended with their parents. At that service, it was decided that if the team won, they would honor God at the end of the game by offering a prayer of thanksgiving near center court. Romar was asked to lead the prayer.

As the game wound down and the victory was secure, Romar was thinking, *Will the players keep the promise they made before the game to honor God?* He was not disappointed. The players kept their promise, and as fifty million people looked on via television, the Bruins and Coach Romar met in a joyful huddle at midcourt, got down on their knees, and bowed their heads. Romar prayed, and his words were overheard by millions of viewers.

That was only the beginning of a unique postgame celebration. The Bruin players did not brag on themselves, but instead took delight in honoring God and their teammates.

What a thrilling moment! Not only was I proud of what the Bruins had accomplished, but I was deeply moved by their gesture of gratitude to the Lord.

Champions Again . . . and Again?

11

So what are the Bruins's chances of repeating as national champs and creating another college basketball dynasty? Well, anything's possible. The Bruins already proved that last season. After twenty years, five coaches, and a program that had seen so many ups and downs it probably could have used an air traffic controller, UCLA is at the top of the collegiate basketball world once again. Of course, staying up there is another matter entirely.

To begin with, it's a different game now than during the last UCLA championship era. The days when one team could dominate completely are harder to find than a parking place in Westwood (which is pretty close to impossible). Just ask the Arkansas Razorbacks what happened to them. The Razor-

backs had every starter back from the team that won the 1994 NCAA title in Charlotte, North Carolina, and they couldn't repeat. The task Arkansas took on looks relatively simple compared to what the Bruins are up against. The challenge UCLA faces is bigger than the roof at Pauley Pavilion.

"We are going to have to grow up fast if we are going to repeat as national champions," Assistant Coach Romar commented.

He knows what he's talking about. Clearly it's not going to be an easy job.

Replacing Ed O'Bannon, Tyus Edney, and George Zidek—three players who were drafted into the NBA (by the New Jersey Nets, Sacramento Kings, and Charlotte Hornets)—doesn't happen overnight. But let's look at some of the Bruins's new prospects for a bright future.

First on the list is Brandon Loyd, a six-footer from Tulsa's Memorial High School. Loyd won the Oklahoma High School Player of the Year award twice before deciding to play his college ball for the Bruins. Experts consider Loyd the best guard to come out of Oklahoma since Mark Price, who played for Georgia Tech and then went on to star in the NBA. Brandon should fit right in because he is a great team player as well as a great shooter.

In UCLA, Loyd sees a program on the rise. "I love the way they play," he told the media, who were curious about why he chose to move to Los Angeles. "Everybody is

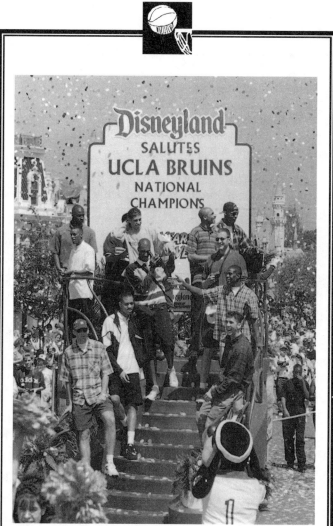
Scott Quintard/ASUCLA

UCLA is located in Westwood, which is not too far from Hollywood, which is not too far from Disneyland. In a show-biz town like Los Angeles, what would seem more natural after winning the Final Four than for the Bruins to say, "We're going to Disneyland" and have a parade with Mickey and a brass band?

unselfish. Everybody plays for the team, and that's the way I've approached basketball all my life."

Loyd has 3-point shooting skills and is also an outstanding student with a 3.5 grade point average.

"I think Brandon is going to open the inside with his shooting for a lot of our slashing and athletic-style players, like Toby Bailey and Charles O'Bannon," said Romar.

Without a doubt, Cameron Dollar will be the starting point guard. After two years of playing against and learning from Edney every day—and another summer of practice and conditioning—Cameron will be one of the leaders of the team.

UCLA is blessed to have three outstanding 6'11" prospects to complete a front line that will no doubt include J. R. Henderson and Charles O'Bannon. Two of them, the hardworking Ike Nwankwo and the highly sought omm'A Givens, were a part of the 1995 championship team. The third is a new recruit, Jelani McCoy.

"Ike is a red-shirted junior who has worked hard in the weight room conditioning his body and working on his footwork," Romar says. He has certainly had the raw talent all along. He was voted the number one high school player in the state of Texas when he played at Cypress Creek near Houston.

With Givens, UCLA won the 1994 recruiting war for the most hotly recruited high school prospect in the country. The 6'11" sophomore didn't get as much playing time as UCLA coaches would have liked in 1995, mainly due to the emergence of Zidek. omm'A is an explosive player who will certainly get an opportunity in the 1996 season.

Jelani McCoy, the third 6'11" player, was a McDonald's All-American when he played at St. Augustine High School in San Diego. Jelani was one of the most coveted players in the nation in 1995.

"Jelani is a gifted frontline player who has a lot of development to do. But he could have an impact right away," said Romar. "He is also very much a team player and unselfish to a fault."

McCoy is tall and thin, but under UCLA's conditioning program, he probably will add the muscle he needs to take the pushing and shoving near the basket.

Kris Johnson, a 6'4" sophomore forward who was overweight and injured in the '95 season, hopes to follow in the footsteps of his father, Marques. (Marques is the former UCLA and NBA star who now announces Bruin games on the radio.)

A former Los Angeles High School City Player of the Year, Kris could be a major contributor. Johnson lost forty pounds during the summer of '95, which made him much quicker. Even though his father was a legend at UCLA, Kris has established his own identity, yet is proud to wear his father's old number, 54.

Kevin Dempsey, a 6'6" forward from San Jose, California, who was one of the Bruins's top seven players as a freshman, could also come back from injuries to make a contribution in 1995-96. Dempsey is a gifted 3-point shooter.

Beyond the expectations from these players, UCLA has four tournament-tested stars in Charles O'Bannon, Bailey, Dollar, and Henderson. Some people close to the team feel that Charles, a player with immense talent, may step into the spotlight now that brother Ed has gone to the pros.

One of the most talented players in the country is J. R. Henderson, who didn't have a great individual game against Arkansas but who played like a veteran through most of his freshman season. Phil Frye, UCLA strength and conditioning coach, said that Henderson has worked hard and put on ten pounds of muscle to withstand the banging a player takes on the front lines.

While UCLA won't have a true classic center like George Zidek in 1995-96, what you might see from the Bruins is the type of play UCLA had between the Abdul-Jabbar and Walton years, in which the front line of Sidney Wicks (6'9"), Curtis Rowe (6'8"), and Steve Patterson (6'9") led the Bruins to two national championships.

UCLA will face a difficult schedule in its bid to repeat. Some of the teams awaiting the defending champion Bruins are Duke, Maryland, Kansas, Louisville, Notre Dame, and UNLV—in addition to opponents in eighteen grueling Pac-10 Conference games.

And so it goes at Westwood, where the expectations are always as high as the blue-and-gold championship banners hanging from the rafters at Pauley. Want to win another championship? Just follow the bouncing ball— from Dollar to Henderson to Bailey to O'Bannon to someone else sent in by the coach waving his rolled up program like a baton.

The players change, but the goal is always the same. The ball is in the air now, so grab it. See where it takes you.

One thing's certain about these Bruins. We already know where they've been. Maybe, just maybe, UCLA is going to get there again.

Scott Quintard/ASUCLA

An upraised "Number One" index finger and an ear-to-ear
smile says it all: The Bruins are champions again.

Appendix

1963-1964

NCAA Championship Season Record: 30-0

Beat Duke 98-83 in NCAA finals at Kansas City

Conference Record: 15-0 (1st)

Starting Lineup:
        F: Jack Hirsch, Sr.
        F: Keith Erickson, Jr.
        C: Fred Slaughter, Sr.
        G: Gail Goodrich, Jr.
        G: Walt Hazzard, Sr. (capt.)

        Coach: John Wooden

First Team All-American:
        Walt Hazzard

First Team All-Conference:
        Walt Hazzard
        Gail Goodrich
        Jack Hirsch

NBA Draft Pick:
        Walt Hazzard, 1st round—Los Angeles Lakers

In NBA:
        Hazzard, 10 years

In UCLA Hall of Fame:
        Walt Hazzard (1984)

1964-1965

NCAA Championship Season Record: 28-2

Beat Michigan 91-80 in NCAA finals at Portland

Conference Record: 14-0 (1st)

Starting Lineup:
        F: Edgar Lacey, So.
        F: Keith Erickson, Sr. (capt.)
        C: Doug McIntosh, Jr.
        G: Gail Goodrich, Sr. (capt.)
        G: Freddie Goss, Jr.

        Coach: John Wooden

First Team All-American:
        Gail Goodrich

First Team All-Conference:
        Gail Goodrich
        Keith Erickson

NBA Draft Pick:
        Gail Goodrich, 1st round—Los Angeles Lakers
        Keith Erickson, 3rd round—San Francisco Warriors

In NBA:
        Goodrich, 14 years
        Erickson, 12 years

In UCLA Hall of Fame:
        Gail Goodrich (1984)
        Keith Erickson (1986)

1965-1966

Season Record: 18-8

Conference Record: 10-4 (2nd)

Starting Lineup:
F: Edgar Lacey, Jr.
F: Mike Lynn, Jr.
C: Doug McIntosh, Sr. (capt.)
G: Mike Warren, So.
G: Kenny Washington, Sr.

Coach: John Wooden

First Team All-Conference:
Mike Lynn

NBA Draft Pick:
Kenny Washington, 8th round—San Francisco
Warriors

In UCLA Hall of Fame:
Mike Warren (1990)

1966-1967

NCAA Championship Season Record: 30-0

Beat Dayton 79-64 in NCAA finals at Louisville

Conference Record: 14-0 (1st)

Starting Lineup:
        F: Lynn Shackelford, So.
        F: Kenny Heitz, So.
        C: Lew Alcindor, So.
        G: Lucius Allen, So.
        G: Mike Warren, Jr. (capt.)

        Coach: John Wooden

First Team All-American:
      Lew Alcindor

First Team All-Conference:
      Lew Alcindor
      Lucius Allen

In UCLA Hall of Fame:
      Lew Alcindor (1984)

1967-1968

NCAA Championship Season Record: 29-1

Beat North Carolina 78-55 in NCAA finals at Los Angeles Sports Arena

Conference Record: 14-0 (1st)

Starting Lineup:
   F: Lynn Shackelford, Jr.
   F: Mike Lynn, Sr.
   C: Lew Alcindor, Jr.
   G: Lucius Allen, Jr.
   G: Mike Warren, Sr. (capt.)

   Coach: John Wooden

First Team All-American:
   Lew Alcindor
   Lucius Allen
   Mike Warren

First Team All-Conference:
   Lew Alcindor
   Mike Warren

NBA Draft Pick:
   Mike Lynn, 4th round—Chicago Bulls
   Edgar Lacey, 4th round—San Francisco Warriors
   Mike Warren, 14th round—Seattle Supersonics

In NBA:
   Lynn, 2 years
   Lacey, 1 year (ABA)

1968-1969

NCAA Championship Season Record: 29-1

Beat Purdue 92-72 in NCAA finals at Louisville

Conference Record: 13-1 (1st)

Starting Lineup:
- F: Lynn Shackelford, Sr. (capt.)
- F: Curtis Rowe, So.
- C: Lew Alcindor, Sr. (capt.)
- G: Kenny Heitz, Sr.
- G: John Vallely, Jr.

Coach: John Wooden

First Team All-American:
Lew Alcindor

First Team All-Conference:
Lew Alcindor
Curtis Rowe

NBA Draft Pick:
Lew Alcindor, #1 selection—Milwaukee Bucks
Lucius Allen, 1st round—Seattle Supersonics
Kenny Heitz, 5th round—Milwaukee Bucks
Bill Sweek, 7th round—Phoenix Suns
Lynn Shackelford, 7th round—Miami Floridians

In NBA:
Alcindor, 20 years
Allen, 10 years
Shackelford, 1 year (ABA)

1969-1970

NCAA Championship Season Record: 28-2

Beat Jacksonville 80-69 in NCAA finals at College Park

Conference Record: 12-2 (1st)

Starting Lineup:
- F: Sidney Wicks, Jr.
- F: Curtis Rowe, Jr.
- C: Steve Patterson, Jr.
- G: John Vallely, Sr. (capt.)
- G: Henry Bibby, So.

Coach: John Wooden

First Team All-American:
Sidney Wicks

First Team All-Conference:
Sidney Wicks

NBA Draft Pick:
John Vallely, 1st round—Atlanta Hawks

In NBA:
Vallely, 2 years

1970-1971

NCAA Championship Season Record: 29-1

Beat Villanova 68-62 in NCAA finals at Houston

Conference Record: 14-0 (1st)

Starting Lineup:
        F: Sidney Wicks, Sr. (capt.)
        F: Curtis Rowe, Sr. (capt.)
        C: Steve Patterson, Sr.
        G: Henry Bibby, Jr.
        G: Kenny Booker, Sr.

        Coach: John Wooden

First Team All-American:
        Sidney Wicks

First Team All-Conference:
        Sidney Wicks
        Curtis Rowe

NBA Draft Pick:
        Sidney Wicks, 1st round—Portland Trailblazers
        Curtis Rowe, 1st round—Detroit Pistons
        Steve Patterson, 2nd round—Cleveland Cavaliers
        Kenny Booker, 14th round—Phoenix Suns

In NBA:
        Wicks, 10 years
        Rowe, 8 years
        Patterson, 5 years

In UCLA Hall of Fame:
        Sidney Wicks (1985)
        Curtis Rowe (1993)

1971-1972

NCAA Championship Season Record: 30-0

Beat Florida State 81-76 in NCAA finals at Los Angeles Sports Arena

Conference Record: 14-0 (1st)

Starting Lineup:
- F: Larry Farmer, Jr.
- F: Keith Wilkes, So.
- C: Bill Walton, So.
- G: Greg Lee, So.
- G: Henry Bibby, Sr. (capt.)

Coach: John Wooden

First Team All-American:
Bill Walton
Henry Bibby

First Team All-Conference:
Bill Walton

NBA Draft Pick:
Henry Bibby, 4th round—New York Knicks

In NBA:
Bibby, 9 years

1972-1973

NCAA Championship Season Record: 30-0

Beat Memphis State 87-66 in NCAA finals at St. Louis

Conference Record: 14-0 (1st)

Starting Lineup:
        F: Larry Farmer, Sr. (capt.)
        F: Keith Wilkes, Jr.
        C: Bill Walton, Jr.
        G: Larry Hollyfield, Sr.
        G: Greg Lee, Jr.

        Coach: John Wooden

First Team All-American:
        Bill Walton
        Keith Wilkes

First Team All-Conference:
        Bill Walton

NBA Draft Pick:
        Swen Nater, 1st round—Milwaukee Bucks
        Larry Hollyfield, 7th round—Portland Trailblazers
        Larry Farmer, 7th round—Cleveland Cavaliers

In NBA:
        Nater, 8 years (3 in ABA)

1973-1974

Season Record: 26-4

Lost to North Carolina State 80-77 (2 OT) in NCAA semifinals at Greensboro

Conference Record: 12-2 (1st)

Starting Lineup:
- F: Dave Myers, Jr.
- F: Keith Wilkes, Sr. (capt.)
- C: Bill Walton, Sr. (capt.)
- G: Greg Lee, Sr.
- G: Tommy Curtis, Sr.

Coach: John Wooden

First Team All-American:
Bill Walton
Keith Wilkes

First Team All-Conference:
Bill Walton
Keith Wilkes

NBA Draft Pick:
Bill Walton, #1 selection—Portland Trailblazers
Keith Wilkes, 1st round—San Francisco Warriors
Tommy Curtis, 7th round—Buffalo Braves
Greg Lee, 7th round—Atlanta Hawks

In NBA:
Walton, 13 years
Wilkes, 12 years
Lee, 2 years (ABA)

In UCLA Hall of Fame:
    Bill Walton (1984)
    Keith Wilkes (1984)

1974-1975

NCAA Championship Season Record: 28-3

Beat Kentucky 92-85 in NCAA finals at San Diego

Conference Record: 12-2 (1st)

Starting Lineup:
> F: Dave Myers, Sr. (capt.)
> F: Marques Johnson, So.
> C: Richard Washington, So.
> G: Andre McCarter, Jr.
> G: Pete Trgovich, Sr.

> Coach: John Wooden

First Team All-American:
> Dave Myers

First Team All-Conference:
> Dave Myers

NBA Draft Pick:
> Dave Myers, 1st round—Los Angeles Lakers
> Pete Trgovich, 3rd round—Detroit Pistons

In NBA:
> Myers, 4 years

In UCLA Hall of Fame:
> Dave Myers (1992)

1975-1976

Season Record: 28-4

Lost to Indiana 65-51 in NCAA semifinals at Philadelphia

Conference Record: 13-1 (1st)

Starting Lineup:
        F: Marques Johnson, Jr. (capt.)
        F: David Greenwood, Fr.
        C: Richard Washington, Jr. (capt.)
        G: Raymond Townsend, So.
        G: Andre McCarter, Sr.

        Coach: Gene Bartow

First Team All-American:
        Richard Washington

First Team All-Conference:
        Richard Washington
        Marques Johnson

NBA Draft Pick:
        Richard Washington, 1st round—Kansas City Kings
        Andre McCarter, 6th round—Kansas City Kings

In NBA:
        Washington, 7 years
        McCarter, 3 years

1976-1977

Season Record: 24-5

Lost to Idaho State 76-75 in NCAA regional first-round game at Provo

Conference Record: 11-3 (1st)

Starting Lineup:
- F: Marques Johnson, Sr. (capt.)
- F: David Greenwood, So.
- C: Bret Vroman, Jr.
- G: Roy Hamilton, So.
- G: Jim Spillane, Sr.

Coach: Gene Bartow

First Team All-American:
Marques Johnson

First Team All-Conference:
Marques Johnson
David Greenwood

NBA Draft Pick:
Marques Johnson, 1st round—Milwaukee Bucks

In NBA:
Johnson, 10 years

In UCLA Hall of Fame:
Marques Johnson (1988)

1977-1978

Season Record: 25-3

Lost to Arkansas 74-70 in NCAA regional first-round game at Albuquerque

Conference Record: 14-0 (1st)

Starting Lineup:
 F: David Greenwood, Jr.
 F: James Wilkes, So.
 C: Gig Sims, So.
 G: Roy Hamilton, Jr.
 G: Raymond Townsend, Sr. (capt.)

 Coach: Gary Cunningham

First Team All-American:
 David Greenwood

First Team All-Conference:
 David Greenwood
 Roy Hamilton
 Raymond Townsend

NBA Draft Pick:
 Raymond Townsend, 1st round—Golden State
 Warriors
 Bret Vroman, 4th round—Philadelphia 76ers
 Ralph Drollinger, 5th round—Seattle Supersonics

In NBA:
 Townsend, 3 years
 Drollinger, 1 year

1978-1979

Season Record: 25-5

Lost to DePaul 95-91 in NCAA regional finals at Provo

Conference Record: 15-3 (1st)

Starting Lineup:
>F: David Greenwood, Sr. (capt.)
>F: Kiki Vandeweghe, Jr.
>C: Gig Sims, Jr.
>G: Roy Hamilton, Sr.
>G: Brad Holland, Sr.

>Coach: Gary Cunningham

First Team All-American:
>David Greenwood

First Team All-Conference:
>David Greenwood
>Roy Hamilton
>Brad Holland

NBA Draft Pick:
>David Greenwood, 1st round—Chicago Bulls
>Roy Hamilton, 1st round—Detroit Pistons
>Brad Holland, 1st round—Los Angeles Lakers

In NBA:
>Greenwood, 12 years
>Hamilton, 2 years
>Holland, 3 years

1979-1980

Season Record: 22-10

Lost to Louisville 59-54 in NCAA finals at Indianapolis

Conference Record: 12-6 (4th)

Starting Lineup:
   F: Kiki Vandeweghe, Sr. (capt.)
   F: James Wilkes, Sr. (capt.)
   C: Mike Sanders, So.
   G: Michael Holton, Fr.
   G: Rod Foster, Fr.

   Coach: Larry Brown

First Team All-Conference:
   Kiki Vandeweghe

NBA Draft Pick:
   Kiki Vandeweghe, 1st round—Dallas Mavericks
   James Wilkes, 3rd round—Chicago Bulls
   Darrell Allums, 5th round—Dallas Mavericks
   Gig Sims, 7th round—Portland Trailblazers

In NBA:
   Vandeweghe, 13 years
   Wilkes, 3 years
   Allums, 1 year

In UCLA Hall of Fame:
   Kiki Vandeweghe (1994)

1980-1981

Season Record: 20-7

Lost to BYU 78-55 in NCAA regional second-round game at Providence

Conference Record: 13-5 (3rd)

Starting Lineup:
- F: Mike Sanders, Jr. (capt.)
- F: Darren Daye, So.
- C: Kenny Fields, Fr.
- G: Michael Holton, So.
- G: Rod Foster, So.

Coach: Larry Brown

First Team All-Conference:
Mike Sanders
Rod Foster

1981-1982

Season Record: 21-6

Conference Record: 14-4 (2nd)

Starting Lineup:
>F: Kenny Fields, So.
>F: Mike Sanders, Sr. (capt.)
>C: Stuart Gray, Fr.
>G: Ralph Jackson, So.
>G: Rod Foster, Jr.

>Coach: Larry Farmer

First Team All-Conference:
>Mike Sanders
>Kenny Fields

NBA Draft Pick:
>Mark Eaton, 4th round—Utah Jazz
>Mike Sanders, 4th round—Kansas City Kings

In NBA:
>Eaton, 11 years
>Sanders, 11 years

1982-1983

Season Record: 23-6

Lost to Utah 67-61 in NCAA regional second-round game at Boise

Conference Record: 15-3 (1st)

Starting Lineup:
> F: Kenny Fields, Jr.
> F: Darren Daye, Sr.
> C: Stuart Gray, So.
> G: Ralph Jackson, Jr.
> G: Rod Foster, Sr.

> Coach: Larry Farmer

First Team All-Conference:
> Kenny Fields
> Rod Foster

NBA Draft Pick:
> Rod Foster, 2nd round—Phoenix Suns
> Michael Holton, 3rd round—Golden State Warriors
> Darren Daye, 3rd round—Washington Bullets

In NBA:
> Holton, 6 years
> Daye, 5 years
> Foster, 3 years

1983-1984

Season Record: 17-11

Conference Record: 10-8 (4th)

Starting Lineup:
        F: Kenny Fields, Sr.
        F: Gary Maloncon, Jr.
        C: Stuart Gray, Jr.
        G: Ralph Jackson, Sr. (capt.)
        G: Montel Hatcher, Fr.

        Coach: Larry Farmer

First Team All-Conference:
        Kenny Fields
        Ralph Jackson

NBA Draft Pick:
        Kenny Fields, 1st round—Milwaukee Bucks
        Stuart Gray, 2nd round—Indiana Pacers
        Ralph Jackson, 4th round—Indiana Pacers

In NBA:
        Fields, 4 years
        Gray, 7 years
        Jackson, 1 year

1984-1985

Season Record: 21-12

Beat Indiana 65-62 in NIT Championship at New York

Conference Record: 12-6 (3rd)

Starting Lineup:
F: Reggie Miller, So.
F: Gary Maloncon, Sr. (capt.)
C: Brad Wright, Sr.
G: Nigel Miguel, Sr.
G: Montel Hatcher, So.

Coach: Walt Hazzard

First Team All-Conference:
Nigel Miguel

NBA Draft Pick:
Brad Wright, 3rd round—Golden State Warriors
Nigel Miguel, 3rd round—New Jersey Nets
Gary Maloncon, 7th round—Los Angeles Clippers

In NBA:
Wright, 2 years

1985-1986

Season Record: 15-14

Conference Record: 9-9 (4th)

Starting Lineup:
- F: Reggie Miller, Jr. (capt.)
- F: Craig Jackson, So.
- C: Jack Haley, Jr.
- G: Montel Hatcher, Jr. (capt.)
- G: Pooh Richardson, Fr.

Coach: Walt Hazzard

First Team All-Conference:
Reggie Miller

1986-1987

Season Record: 25-7

Lost to Wyoming 78-68 in NCAA regional second-round game at Salt Lake City

Conference Record: 14-4 (1st)

Starting Lineup:
  F: Reggie Miller, Sr. (capt.)
  F: Charles Rochelin, So.
  C: Jack Haley, Sr.
  G: ave Immel, Jr.
  G: Pooh Richardson, So.

  Coach: Walt Hazzard

First Team All-Conference:
  Reggie Miller
  Pooh Richardson

NBA Draft Pick:
  Reggie Miller, 1st round—Indiana Pacers
  Jack Haley, 4th round—Chicago Bulls
  Montel Hatcher, 7th round—Indiana Pacers

1987-1988

Season Record: 16-14

Conference Record: 12-6 (2nd)

Starting Lineup:
        F: Craig Jackson, Sr. (capt.)
        F: Trevor Wilson, So.
        C: Kelvin Butler, Sr.
        G: Dave Immel, Sr. (capt.)
        G: Pooh Richardson, Jr.

        Coach: Walt Hazzard

First Team All-Conference:
        Pooh Richardson
        Trevor Wilson

1988-1989

Season Record: 21-10

Lost to North Carolina 88-81 in NCAA regional second-round game at Atlanta

Conference Record: 13-5 (3rd)

Starting Lineup:
        F: Trevor Wilson, Jr.
        F: Don MacLean, Fr.
        C: Kevin Walker, Jr.
        G: Darrick Martin, Fr.
        G: Pooh Richardson, Sr. (capt.)

        Coach: Jim Harrick

First Team All-Conference:
        Pooh Richardson
        Trevor Wilson

NBA Draft Pick:
        Pooh Richardson, 1st round—Minnesota
            Timberwolves

1989-1990

Season Record: 22-11

Lost to Duke 90-81 in NCAA regional first-round game at East Rutherford

Conference Record: 11-7 (4th)

Starting Lineup:
   F: Trevor Wilson, Sr. (capt.)
   F: Don MacLean, So.
   F: Tracy Murray, Fr.
   G: Darrick Martin, So.
   G: Gerald Madkins, So.

   Coach: Jim Harrick

First Team All-Conference:
   Don MacLean
   Trevor Wilson

NBA Draft Pick:
   Trevor Wilson, 2nd round—Atlanta Hawks

1990-1991

Season Record: 23-9

Lost to Penn State 74-69 in NCAA regional first-round game at Syracuse

Conference Record: 11-7 (2nd)

Starting Lineup:
F: Don MacLean, Jr.
F: Tracy Murray, So.
F: Mitchell Butler, So.
G: Darrick Martin, Jr.
G: Gerald Madkins, Jr.

Coach: Jim Harrick

First Team All-Conference:
Don MacLean

1991-1992

Season Record: 28-5

Lost to Indiana 106-79 in NCAA regional finals at
Albuquerque

Conference Record:16-2 (1st)

Starting Lineup:
        F: Don MacLean, Sr.
        F: Tracy Murray, Jr.
        G: Mitchell Butler, Jr.
        G: Gerald Madkins, Sr. (capt.)
        G: Shon Tarver, So.

        Coach: Jim Harrick

First Team All-American:
      Don MacLean

First Team All-Conference:
      Don MacLean
      Tracy Murray

NBA Draft Pick:
      Tracy Murray, 1st round—San Antonio Spurs
      Don MacLean, 1st round—Detroit Pistons

1992-1993

Season Record: 22-11

Lost to Michigan 86-84 (OT) in NCAA regional second-round game at Tucson

Conference Record: 11-7 (3rd)

Starting Lineup:
      F: Mitchell Butler, Sr. (capt.)
      F: Ed O'Bannon, So.
      C: Richard Petruska, Sr.
      G: Shon Tarver, Jr.
      G: Tyus Edney, So.

      Coach: Jim Harrick

First Team All-Conference:
      Ed O'Bannon
      Tyus Edney

NBA Draft Pick:
      Richard Petruska, 2nd round—Houston Rockets

1993-1994

Season Record: 21-7

Lost to Tulsa 112-102 in NCAA regional first-round game at Oklahoma City

Conference Record: 13-5 (2nd)

Starting Lineup:
        F: Ed O'Bannon, Jr.
        F: Charles O'Bannon, Fr.
        C: George Zidek, Jr.
        G: Tyus Edney, Jr.
        G: Shon Tarver, Sr. (capt.)

        Coach: Jim Harrick

First Team All-Conference:
        Ed O'Bannon
        Tyus Edney

About the Author

Keith Erickson was a starter on UCLA's first two NCAA Championship basketball teams under Coach John Wooden. He played on the U.S. Olympic volleyball team in Tokyo, Japan, in 1964 and played in the NBA twelve years. A speaker and sports-TV analyst, he currently lives in Santa Monica. He is married and the father of five children.